Funding & Financial Execution

for Early-Stage Companies

The number one knowledge source for entrepreneurs focused on creating and retaining company value.

Rod Hoagland

QUICKSILVER
CFO CONSULTING

Editorial Advisory Board

Entrepreneurial Finance Experts

Acknowledgments

My sincere thanks to the many entrepreneurs, investors and mentors who have helped me grow. The members of the editorial advisory board have been very helpful in helping me complete this project. Laura Raynak collaborated on the Intelligent Staffing chapter and all others have provided valuable review notes and advice. Special thanks also to Bill Musgrave, CEO of The Enterprise Network (TEN) and the member companies who have allowed me to use the incubator as a laboratory while writing this book.

Table of Contents

Section Two - Early-Stage Financial Execution

Introduction

A venture business combines both high risk and the potential for high reward; successful venture entrepreneurs work consistently at increasing the size of the prize and reducing the risk.

Entrepreneurs can learn a lot from this simple concept. Technology is only valuable if someone is *compelled* to use it, and a steady, otherwise good business may not present a large enough prize to be worthy of significant risk. Simply stated as it is, this concept is the driving message contained within Funding & Financial Execution for Early-Stage Companies.

I have been both delighted and saddened over the years. Delighted from the many times I have worked with entrepreneurs who were able to create a valuable, sustainable venture business and as a result were able to claim a sizeable reward from the financial marketplace. I have also been saddened when I observed entrepreneurs who failed to align their company with this concept. A few entrepreneurs spent many long days and months, sometimes years, without being able to build investor interest in their early-stage company. Some entrepreneurs were able to obtain an audience from a venture capitalist, but were unable to guide the funding process to completion. Other entrepreneurs successfully raised venture capital but found themselves unable to leverage the initial investment into a sustainable venture business.

Armed with these experiences I decided to embark on an ambitious goal—concisely communicate to entrepreneurs my knowledge on how to attract venture funding, and how to leverage the funding into a valuable, sustainable venture business. As I wrote, I augmented and honed my knowledge through interviews and other primary research with entrepreneurs, money sources and other seasoned consultants. I concluded the most successful communication approach would first view the issues from the 40,000-foot level, but truly communicate take home value useful to the entrepreneur at the 5,000 to 10,000-foot level. Funding & Financial Execution for Early Stage Companies blends the big picture strategy overview with the actual wining tactics that entrepreneurs need.

For the entrepreneur to put these strategies and tactics to use successfully, he or she must understand that each topic requires a combination of three approaches—art, science and wisdom—to gain true knowledge.

The art of finance is the application of funding, planning and execution tactics to practical use, i.e. the right brain integration of how finance interacts with the broader business model and business plan. Conversely, the science of finance provides a mathematical framework in which to analyze individual topics quantitatively. However this is not a mathematics textbook, and I have tried to present the math precisely at the level necessary for the entrepreneur. Still, neither of these approaches is enough for an entrepreneur to be truly successful, as he or she still must acquire a keen sense of judgment that has been built through the wisdom of experience. Together all three approaches generate a practical, pragmatic and executable roadmap.

Funding & Financial Execution for Early-Stage Companies is organized into two sections. "Section One – Early-Stage Planning and Funding" starts with an introduction of why shareholder value is important, what influences early-stage company value, and in the process, which of these influences the entrepreneur can control and which ones he or she cannot. I discuss the funding decision from the viewpoint of the venture investor. Successive chapters of Section One walk the entrepreneur through the remainder of the planning and fundraising processes: financial planning, capital planning, investor targeting, alternatives to equity financing, understanding term sheets and due diligence. Twenty-one myths about funding are given as a final recap of the section.

"Section Two – Early-Stage Financial Execution" focuses on the key financial execution issues confronting the entrepreneur—maximizing the benefit from and allocation of financial resources with a view towards intelligently staffing the early-stage company, stock options traps and tricks, steps to establishing a baseline financial control structure, and a concluding discussion of seven hard learned lessons.

Section One

Early-Stage Planning and Funding

Influencing Early-Stage Company Valuations —the Art Behind the Science

Why Start this Book with a Chapter On Influencing Shareholder Value?

The answer to this question has two reasons behind it. First, every early-stage entrepreneur struggles with the fundamental question—*what is the value of our company?* The first early-stage high technology company I experienced firsthand was a little known laser technology start-up called Uniphase (now part of JDS Uniphase). My graduate entrepreneurship course project studied the business plan of this company. The Uniphase executives clearly pondered the same question—*what is the value of our company*? Twenty some years latter, early-stage entrepreneurs still struggle with the answer, as will entrepreneurs twenty years from now.

The second reason is this: if you want to attract investment in your company you have to demonstrate how you are going to grow shareholder value. Although most venture investors have a strong humanistic side, the bottom line is, when they invest money in an early-stage company the goal is to make more money, i.e. they must believe the investment will increase in value.

This perspective is not meant to diminish the concept of customer value, quite the opposite, as I believe shareholder value and customer value are sustainable only when both come together in a company. Such a company succeeds in building customer value and can only continue to do so when it shows increased shareholder value to attract more capital, therefore allowing through additional investment the creation of additional customer value. Likewise creation of shareholder value depends on customer value: somebody must buy your product or service.

The Purpose of a Business Plan, Business Model and Value Proposition

As early-stage companies have not yet demonstrated significant customer value, shareholder value is based upon the promise of the business plan. The diagrams on the following pages provide visual illustrations of these concepts.

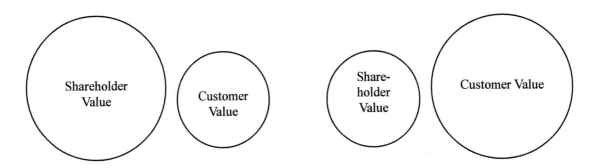

Dysfunctional Relationships Between Shareholder and Customer Value

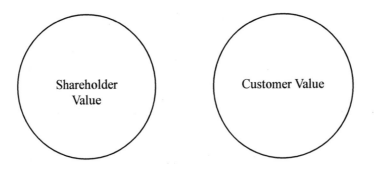

Equilibrium Relationship Between Shareholder and Customer Value - The Basis for Dual Maximization

Business Plan

Environmental Analysis

Financial Markets	Market Size & Growth	Market Needs	Competitors

Conceptual Models

Business Model	Value Proposition

Execution Plans

Capital Plan	Tech-nology Plan	Marketing Plan		
		Channel Plan	Pricing Strategy	Sales Plan

Financial Plan

Staffing Plan

Values Maximized

Shareholder Value	Customer Value

A well conceived business plan combines the environmental analyses, two simple but powerful conceptual models, and supporting detailed execution plans. The underlying purpose of the business plan is to show how you integrate these three elements—the environmental analysis, conceptual models, and the execution plans—to maximize customer and shareholder value.

The genesis of any well defined business plan starts with an analysis of the surrounding environment. On the shareholders' side of the analysis are the market size and growth, tempered by the current financial market conditions and perceptions. Without a sizeable market represented either by an established market undergoing change or an embryonic market with high growth, substantive shareholder value cannot be built. Conversely, in the customer value analysis, the company must serve market needs that are not and will not be adequately addressed by competitors.

The second stage of the business plan development is to create and present the conceptual models. One conceptual model, the value proposition, illustrates how customers will receive value. The most powerful value propositions typically show how a customer's time and costs are reduced, and benefits increase through the delivery of Return on Investment (ROI) and not merely the enablement of ROI.

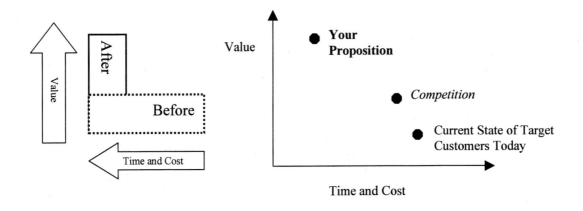

Powerful Value Propositions

The second conceptual model is the business model. In reviewing popular business literature I find several types of business models, but seldom do I find a clear definition of what a business model is. In discussions with colleagues I have heard several definitions and finally concluded that a common, consensual definition of the business model really does not exist. However, two definitions I have heard do set the stage for a short meaningful discussion.

The first definition comes from Horst E. Lehrheuer of CommonGoal Consulting, "The business model is a simplified description of the value creation and capturing system of a business." The second definition comes from *Internet Business Models and Strategies* (Allan Afuah and Christopher Tucci, McGraw Hill, 2001, pages 3-4); "The first determinant of a firm's performance is its business model. This is the method by which a firm builds and uses its resources to offer its customers better value than its competitors and to make money doing so. It details how a firm makes money now and how it plans to do so in the long term. The model is what enables a firm to have a sustainable competitive advantage, to perform better than its rivals in the long term. A business model can be conceptualized as a system that is made up of components, linkages between the components, and dynamics."

I believe these are good workable definitions provided that the entrepreneur is given some additional framework to build upon. First, the purpose of a business model is to show how the company intends to increase shareholder value, or more broadly, how value is produced and allocated across the entire stakeholder chain—customers, partners, shareholders, employees, suppliers and so on. The primary allocation of the value created is performed through manipulation of the price obtained and the risk assumed. Second, the components of the business model reflect the core company strategy that leads to value creation. The business model components reflect not only the classic marketing decisions, but also development, manufacturing, organizational and financial decisions.

The classic marketing decisions start with the traditional "four P's"—Product, Place, Promotion and Price. Over the years many more P's have been added—including Pre- and Post-sales support, Positioning, Publicity, etc. Marketing decisions also include some C's—primarily Customer, Competition and Channel. Development decisions start with a classic make (develop internally) versus buy (acquire or license) decision and continue with how to make or how to buy decisions. Manufacturing decisions include where and how the manufacturing is done—locally, internationally, internally, or contracted and on the fixed versus variable cost volume levels. Organizational decisions include the method of support provided to customers, skill levels of the employee base and vertical versus horizontal management structures. Likewise financial decisions such as the amount of debt leverage and the breakeven versus market share objective also influence the overall business model.

We can therefore say the business model represents the combination of all core decisions related to the performance of the business enterprise, which combine to create or destroy value, and the allocation of the resulting net value between customers, shareholders, employees and suppliers based primarily upon price and risk.

Entrepreneurs who are reading carefully noticed that the preceding paragraph also included the concept of *value destruction*. Incorrect business model components may in fact destroy value for all companies including the early-stage company. The task in developing a business plan is to optimize all business model components to create maximum value, a process that is much easier said than done. In most startups, management attempts to achieve a "good enough" business model while simultaneously addressing hosts of other distractions. I believe it should also be understood that some business model components create value for more than one constituency, e.g. contract manufacturing reduces your capital investment and increases time to revenue, therefore this decision can add value to the supplier, the shareholder and the customer.

My purpose in this brief business model overview is to highlight the importance of a viable business model in the investment decision by a potential investor. If the business model does not show how value is created by the business, then your ability to attract funding is severely diminished—the business model functions as a litmus test on the funding decision. The best method for creating a winning business model is to start with your initial assumptions and test, modify, retest and re-modify the assumptions with many advisors, customers and potential investors. Many forward thinking experts, like John C. Gale of Taligo LLC, insist that the process of developing a one page graphic representation of a company's business model causes the company to think through crucial issues. The graphic shows the various business cycle participants and how funds, product, and information flow between them.

Supporting these two conceptual models are the execution plans. A few sub-plans, namely the financial and staffing plans are 'horizontal'. These plans illustrate how available resources, cash and the largest use of cash, staffing, will be allocated across the different functions of the company to build up shareholder and customer value. A decision to use cash or staffing resources in one functional area requires a decision not to use those resources in other, perhaps equally important areas.

On the other hand most other execution plans are 'vertical' in nature. Within a specific functional area they detail, based on the allocated resources, how the company will execute the function. Although there are interdependencies within these vertical execution plans, the interdependencies do not represent either/or decisions between functional areas. The marketing and related plans, the technology plan and the capital plan are prime examples of these vertical execution plans.

So it is within this context that we must begin to examine what exactly influences shareholder value as a prelude to the funding process. The second chapter will discuss the horizontal financial plan, what its key drivers are, how the financial plan supports and interacts with the rest of the business plan, and illustrates the level of funding required. The remaining chapters of Section One outline the capital plan (matching funding to milestone achievement and cash needs), investor targeting, alternatives to equity, understanding term sheets, the due diligence process and common myths on funding.

Although this book does not directly discuss the technology and marketing plans in detail, considerable attention is given to how these plans integrate into the capital plan, the financial plan and the shareholder value equation.

Assessing Organizational Value

Assessing organizational value requires the skillful combination of art (qualitative factors) and science (quantitative factors). In this chapter I look primarily at the qualitative factors that influence the "total enterprise value" of an early-stage company from the viewpoint of the venture capital investor seeking to acquire a *pro rata* equity share of the company. Total enterprise value in this context is different from a "controlling value" or "minority value" that would be assigned by another investor with other motives. Simply put, someone with a controlling value or minority value motivation measures how much a company is worth to them using a yardstick quite different from that of the venture investor.

Many unseasoned entrepreneurs also do not rigorously think through a basic valuation equation—money received from an investor divided by the percentage of the company required, less the investment, must equal your pre-money valuation (the pre-money valuation is the company value you and the investor agree upon before they invest their money). For example an investment of $1M for 20% of the company implies the company is worth $4M before the investment. The following tables illustrate this point.

$$\text{Implicit Pre-Money Valuation} = \left(\frac{\text{Funds Invested}}{\text{Percentage of Company Obtained}} \right) - \text{Funds Invested}$$

Implicit Pre-Money Valuation Equation

Implicit Pre-Money Valuation ($000's)

(Derived as a function of funds invested and ownership percentage obtained.)

Funding Round Size		Ownership Percentage Sold 10%	15%	Frequent Percentage Range 20%	25%	30%	35%	40%
Frequent Seed Round Size	$ 50	450	283	200	150	117	93	75
	$ 100	900	567	400	300	233	186	150
	$ 250	2,250	1,417	1,000	750	583	464	375
	$ 500	4,500	2,833	2,000	1,500	1,167	929	750
Frequent Second Round Size	$ 750	6,750	4,250	3,000	2,250	1,750	1,393	1,125
	$ 1,000	9,000	5,667	4,000	3,000	2,333	1,857	1,500
	$ 1,500	13,500	8,500	6,000	4,500	3,500	2,786	2,250
Frequent Third Round Size	$ 2,000	18,000	11,333	8,000	6,000	4,667	3,714	3,000
	$ 2,500	22,500	14,167	10,000	7,500	5,833	4,643	3,750
	$ 3,000	27,000	17,000	12,000	9,000	7,000	5,571	4,500
	$ 4,000	36,000	22,667	16,000	12,000	9,333	7,429	6,000
	$ 5,000	45,000	28,333	20,000	15,000	11,667	9,286	7,500

Projected Ownership of Common Shareholders

(Derived as a function of the number of investment rounds and average percentage ownership sold per investment round.)

Ownership Percentage Sold Round Number	10%	15%	Frequent Percentage Range 20%	25%	30%	35%	40%
Seed Round	90%	85%	80%	75%	70%	65%	60%
Second Round	81%	72%	64%	56%	49%	42%	36%
Third Round	73%	61%	51%	42%	34%	27%	22%
Fourth Round	66%	52%	41%	32%	24%	18%	13%
Fifth Round	59%	44%	33%	24%	17%	12%	8%
Sixth Round	53%	38%	26%	18%	12%	8%	5%

Even though the primary purpose of this chapter is to discuss the qualitative factors influencing the total enterprise value, the framework established by quantitative valuation methods provides a useful foundation for discussion.

The Science – Quantitative Methods

There are three basic mathematical methods used to establish the valuation of a non-public company. The first method focuses on a discounted projection of the company's future cash flow or economic earning value. The second method draws upon an alignment against market comparables. The third method, which often does not apply to early-stage high technology companies, relies on an analysis of the company's net asset fair market value. No one method is superior for all occasions, and quite commonly, a potential early stage investor considers elements drawn from all three methods to determine a pre-money valuation.

$$\text{Net Present Value} = \text{Summation Over n Periods} \left[\frac{n^{\text{th}} \text{ Period Economics Earnings}}{\left(\text{One} + \text{Discount Rate}\right)^{\text{Raised to the } n^{\text{th}} \text{ Power}}} \right]$$

The Classic Discount Valuation Formula (Net Present Value)

The Art – Qualitative Factors

Although the science of valuations creates a useful and necessary foundation, the art of valuations dominates the science. As an illustration, the discounted projection of a company's future cash flow seeks to quantify the company's attributes in financial terms, and then discounts the projection based on judgmental financial risk premium adjustments. Judgment is the key premise, as one person's judgment is often extremely different from that of another. Judgment is also an inherent attribute of the market comparables method, starting with the market's perception of equity investments, fine-tuned by a more specific perception of that industry, and subsequently tuned by the potential investor's decisions on how to align the individual company against the market comparables. The potential investor also considers the unsystematic downside risk; if the company stumbles, what solid net and intangible assets are available for investment recovery, will anyone purchase them, and if so who receives the proceeds? Thus all three methods have been combined, each method relying upon the judgment of the individual creating the valuation.

Given that the underlying "judgment premise" is common to all three valuation methods, most early-stage company management teams are better served by understanding how to influence the judgment factors, as opposed to attempting their own valuation calculations. The often quoted caveat "the value is the price a willing buyer and a willing seller agree upon" is very appropriate. How you mold the company, and how you package the company for sale to an investor, enhances or detracts from the ultimate valuation in the eyes of a willing investor.

There are a few specific cases an early-stage company should consider a formal independent valuation, for example:

- The company has experienced a disaster and needs to pursue an insurance claim or legal action.
- The company has had a significant time elapse since its last preferred financing and needs an independent valuation of its common stock price to fix option grant prices.
- A sale of the company is contemplated and the company has dissenting shareholders.

But, assuming these unusual events do not fit your case, prepare yourself to plan and execute an active approach to influencing the potential investor's valuation judgments.

The following paragraphs guide you in developing and executing this proactive approach by highlighting the management, technology, and market/marketing assessment factors, discussing financial risk premiums, and illustrating the management's motivational situations that affect valuation judgments.

Assessment Factors

Each of these answers affects future required investment assumptions and risk.

Assessing the technological, management and market parameters provides the context supporting the financial plan as well as developing an initial set of financial risk premium adjustments. An underlying theme to this discussion is can you really build a successful company, and why can you do it better than anyone else?

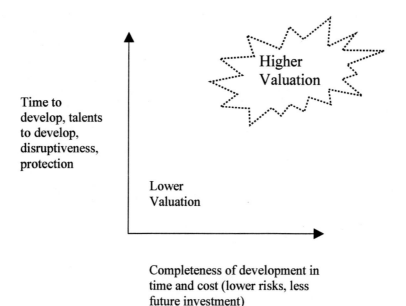

Time to develop, talents to develop, disruptiveness, protection

Higher Valuation

Lower Valuation

Completeness of development in time and cost (lower risks, less future investment)

Visual Representation of Technology Assessment Factors

The technology assessment begins with questions like the following:

- How disruptive is the technology?
- How developed is the technology; i.e. is it theoretical, proven, or utilized by paying customers?
- How sustainable is the technology - what talents were necessary for the development, are they commonly available, and how long did it take to develop the technology?
- Is the technology protected or can it be protectable by patents or copyrights - how clean is the protection from other infringement claims?
- What issues impact the scalability of the technology and cost reduction assumptions?

Each of these answers affects the future required investment assumptions and risk. An accurate description of the technology status should neither overplay nor underplay your present and future requirements.

Overplaying reflects poorly on management's judgment and credibility; underplaying deflates the valuation and is viewed as a sign of management's inability to market the company and communicate clearly.

Technology Assessment	Management Assessment	Market Assessment
• Disruptive? • Developed? • Scaleable? • Sustainable? • Protected?	• Complete? • Experienced? • Flexible/Adaptable? • Marketplace Awareness? • Team Functionality?	• Market Size & Growth? • Dependent Events? • Marketing Plan Elements? • Competitive Threats?

↓

Financial Risk Premiums
- Profit and Cash Flow Potential?
- Total Investment Required?
- Negative Event Vulnerability?
- Liquidity Time Horizon?
- Liquidity Path?

↓

Motivational Adjustments
- Multiple Potential Leads?
- Immediate Cash Requirement?
- Investment Alternatives?
- What Sector Is "Hot?"

↓

Structural Terms

↓

Pre-Money Valuation Offer

Early-Stage Company Valuation Model

Assessing management also begins with similar questions about current status and future requirements:

- How complete is the management team; do they recognize the holes?
- How experienced is the management team; have they learned on someone else's money; can they execute the business plan?
- How flexible is the management team; will they bring in more experienced executives in key roles if required?
- Is the management team seeking and answering the tough questions; do they understand the market space?
- Can the management team sell the company to new employees and executive talent?
- Does the team really function as a team?

These are tough questions to answer honestly if your own ego is on the line. The investor wants to know your constitution, or "mindset"—are you "at peace" with controlling and owning a smaller slice of a larger total pie, or are you determined to have the largest slice possible at the expense of growing the size of the total pie?

Assessing the market is closely tied to assessing the marketing plan. Attacking a large market without a well thought out plan does not work, but at least you can fix the plan. Attacking a small market with an excellent plan will not provide the payoff a venture investor requires. Therefore a key market assessment question is how large is the market today, and how fast is it growing? Another key market assessment question is "what other external market events are you dependent upon for your product to be useable?"

> *Attacking a large market without a well thought out plan does not work, but at least you can fix the plan. Attacking a small market with an excellent plan will not provide the payoff a venture investor requires.*

Marketing plan assessments look at how your company will exploit the market. Have you picked the appropriate positioning, market entry and customer entry segments, channel strategy and pricing formulas? You will be asked other forward-looking questions like these:

- How long will it take to develop the necessary strategy evidence?
- What will be your sales cycle (time to sell, time to deploy, time to customer competence, time to customer value realization)?
- Is your segment-leveraging model viable?
- What competitive threats exist?

Many early-stage companies fail to develop, test, redevelop and retest their marketing plan thoroughly.

The list of assessment questions outlined above is by no means exhaustive. Many more assessment questions could be asked, and as result of all of these questions the management team's heads may spin while they forget or fail to focus on key points. A good team will guard against becoming unfocussed and will take the approach of identifying and achieving the most important objectives possible within the available resource constraints, as opposed to achieving a little of everything and all of nothing.

Financial Risk Premiums

Many financial risk premiums are a natural outgrowth of the assessment process, as the assessment process drives the financial plan of the company, outlining the perimeter of the "financial box:"

- What is the trade-off decision between market share accumulation (increased sales at a high cost structure) and financial break-even points?
- How much total investment is required to achieve the business plan?
- What is the true profit potential?
- How vulnerable is the company to negative events (competitive threats, new technology, market conditions, technical achievements, internal politics)?
- Are multiple liquidation paths considered - or is management predisposed to the IPO track only?

The financial risk premium currently associated with the first question is heavily influenced by factors external to the company. Pursuing a market share accumulation strategy when the investment community is focused on survivability (low cash burn and faster break-even points) can increase the financial risk premium. Therefore, understanding the current financial market mindset, and deciding if you agree, creates a feedback loop to fundamental business plan assumptions.

However, there is one other key financial risk premium that does not flow directly from the company's financial plan and cannot be directly influenced by the company – is the liquidation window big (generous) and open (e.g. what is the state of the IPO and M&A markets)? If we go back to the net present value formula outlined earlier in this chapter, a potential investor considers the time their money is tied up in the investment, therefore the number of periods the potential investor considers plausible is generally less than five years. Correspondingly, the future cash flow measured is the investors' liquidation payout(s). Both of these factors are built upon the earnings potential of the company and a consideration of the current financial markets. In completing the variables in an investor's net present value equation, historically the discount rate used by venture capital firms ranges from 25% to 50%, depending upon the venture capitalist's internal hurdle rate and the company's maturity (e.g. time to profit, time to liquidity).

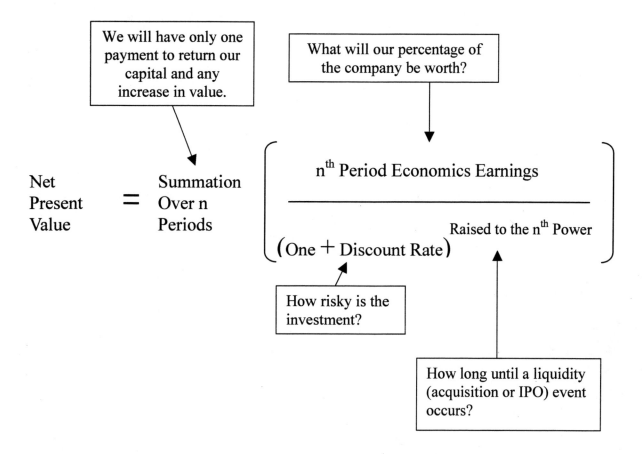

Net Present Value from a Venture Investors Perspective

Some of the best sources for keeping in touch with current funding market dynamics include the quarterly *Money Tree Survey* published by PriceWaterhouseCoopers (www.pwcmoneytree.com), the two page *Business Outlook* Column in Business Week, continuing coverage in the Wall Street Journal, and Venture Wire (www.venturewire.com).

The potential investor also correlates the financial risk premium to the probability of success. If the probability of success drops significantly below one hundred percent and the potential market opportunity is not extremely high, the valuation drops to zero, as the potential investor is not a willing investor.

Motivational Adjustments

The caveat "the value is the price a willing buyer and a willing seller agree upon" was brought up earlier in this chapter. Common sense, so why repeat it again here? Because many management teams forget to consider a few basic ways that caveat influences the pre-money valuation of their company. The potential investor asks, "Has the company effectively marketed itself to other lead investors?"

> **Has the company effectively marketed themselves to other potential lead investors?**

If no other lead investors are in the bidding, then the pre-money valuation can probably be lower and still accepted. Of course once a "no-shop" clause is agreed upon, the company must make every effort to comply, but before then, have you aggressively created multiple lead investor demand? However, also keep in mind that "over-shopping" can also lead to decreased demand.

Second, how quickly does the company need the funding? A high burn rate coupled with a low cash balance is not only a sign of management myopia, but if current investors also signal that they are unwilling or unable to back the company further without other new investors, which way do you think the pre-money valuation will be adjusted? In some cases the current investors just cannot or will not participate without a new investor: do yourself a favor and avoid overtly sending this signal. Some companies consciously or unconsciously decide to run cash down as far as they can while trying to achieve milestones. For some companies the risk produces an acceptable increase in the pre-money valuation, but the risk can and will destroy the company if you are wrong.

Another motivational adjustment factor in pre-money valuations that management teams frequently miss is the alternative choice some potential investors must consider. Investors who have large established funds may not be able to focus on early-stage companies because of their own partner bandwidth or because earlier investments require more funds as a result of a slowdown in achieving liquidity events. Some venture funds also must work within charter restrictions of their limited partners, whose ability to stand behind funding commitments to the venture fund have been hurt by changes in the financial markets. Alternatively, investors may have already placed an investment in your market space or other potential early-stage investments may just appear more promising, either based on the company fundamentals or because they are in the currently hot sector and your company is not.

Structural Terms

Many inexperienced management teams, in hindsight, consider some common venture investment structural terms as "valuation tricks." I include in this category warrants, oversized option pools, ratchet adjustments, accumulating dividends and super liquidation preferences. All of these structural terms are explained in detail in Chapter Five – "Understanding Term Sheets." Right now the purpose for bringing up the structural terms is to explain that these structural terms can increase the stated pre-money valuation at the expense of future dilution, therefore effectively increasing the investor's total equity position and decreasing the true pre-money valuation of the company or by adversely impacting common shareholder participation in the proceeds from an acquisition.

Clearly some management teams knowingly accept adverse structural terms as a trade-off for pre-money valuation boasting rights, because they are willing to trade potential future dilution for less dilution today, or because they have executed poor investor marketing and negotiations. But I have never seen the next-round term sheet contain fewer complications than the previous round. Therefore, consider not only the baseline these terms set for future rounds, but also the negotiations involved if the next-round investor requires a modification to the Stockholder's Rights Agreement.

Conclusion

Investors invest money to make more money. Therefore they must believe in your company's ability to build both shareholder and customer value. Correctly done, the business plan illustrates a keen understanding of the business environment, a strong business model and value proposition, and a credible understanding of the execution required.

Early-stage company value is the outcome of a synergistic blend of technology, management and market, all of which are assessed by the potential investor. A weak link in any of the assessment factors, financial risk premiums, or management motivational adjustments has a negative effect on an investor's judgment concerning your pre-money valuation. An effective plan and execution strategy will recognize and focus on the factors that management can influence, seeking to create the proper balance of focus and added value available within the resource constraints. Although you cannot influence the current funding environment on a macro level you must be aware of the current funding environment to understand how your business plan should be appropriately molded and aimed. Be mindful of putting yourself in a weak-negotiating position by failing to target an appropriate size investor audience or by not maintaining a conservative fallback cash position. Finally, consider the trade-offs inherent in pumping the pre-money valuation at the expense of dilutive financing terms.

Developing a Financial Plan for a Start-Up Company

Many new companies try to develop their first financial plan as a quick last-minute exercise performed just prior to a presentation for potential investors. Although "winging it" is sometimes a necessary skill for entrepreneurs, improvising with the financial plan shortchanges the financial plan's value as an integral component of a solid business plan. Since the lack of knowledge usually slows the integration of the financial plan into the overall business plan, this chapter explores how to bridge that knowledge gap.

Comparing Complexities in Start-Up and Mature Companies

Developing a financial plan for a start-up company is different from creating a financial plan for an established enterprise. Organizations involve distinct complications at various stages of their evolution. With a start-up company the primary complexity is proper coordination of the business plan into a financial picture, i.e. the financial plan. A secondary complexity is in keeping the plan very flexible, yet simple, in order to be responsive to changes in the business plan assumptions.

In contrast, an established business enterprise already has in place product pricing and cost structure, a revenue stream with more accurate predictive capacity and a substantial staff. The established company's complexities include affairs like internal coordination between multiple divisions, departments, and corporate functions. In addition, set policies such as internal hurdle rates, return on assets and return on equity are often imposed on the internal operating units. As a result, the coordination becomes focused on standardization of the plan between divisions and departments, allocation discussions between functions, internal due dates, hiding and uncovering "honey pots" or "cookie jars," and hurdle requirements for the final plan. These all combine to reflect a preset bottom-line performance target.

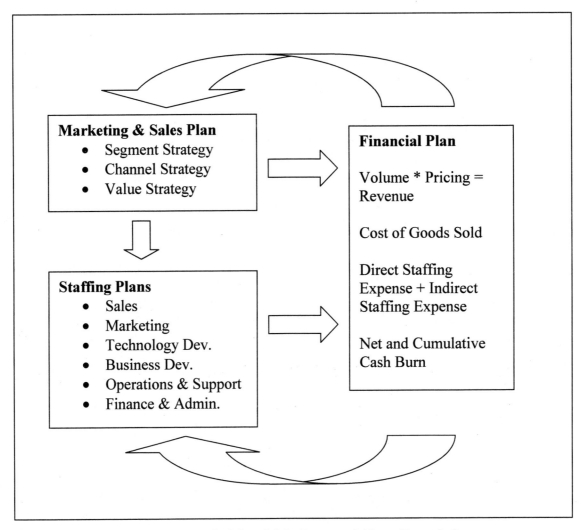

Business Plan Critical Links and Feedback Loops

The Feedback Loop Between the Financial Plan and the Business Plan

As mentioned above, a start-up company's financial plan must be an accurate reflection of its business plan. Neither the business plan nor the reflective financial plan can be created in isolation; i.e. business plan assumptions cause financial consequences. In turn, the financial consequences signal the need — sometimes quietly, sometimes loudly — to modify the business plan assumptions. Key results of the financial plan, such as total cash burn and highest burn rate, guide the company to the level of external funding required.

Determining the Appropriate Time Horizon of the Detailed Financial Plan

Along with milestones outlined in your business plan, external factors will highlight the appropriate time horizon your detailed financial plan should cover. For example:

- What are the major milestones of product development?
- What are the realistic expectations for market penetration times?
- What are the funding trends in the venture capital community?
- Is there a point when expenses will need to increase significantly?

In most cases the ideal horizon is not less than twelve months and not more than twenty-four months. Less than twelve months suggests an underdeveloped business plan. More than twenty-four months is an unrealistic period to believe in your own accuracy. Whichever time horizon you select, be prepared to modify it as necessary — as time passes and your business plan and financial plan are put through dependent development cycles.

Revenue Assumptions

The company's revenue assumptions make up a key part of the financial plan. The classic price and volume revenue equation cannot be answered with credibility until other key marketing questions are explored. Some of these questions are:

> *... if you have done your marketing homework, then you are ready to create a monthly extrapolation of the price, quantity and resulting revenue expectations.*

- What are the reference and channel goals over the time horizon of the financial plan?

25

- If you have a complex, costly software application, are you searching for development partners with the goal of reference over revenue (and does your Board of Directors agree)?
- What is your beta test plan? Does it have firm start and end goals?
- If you plan to use channel partners, what will it take to bring the channel partners up to capacity, and what channel discounts are expected?
- Will you need to offer exclusivity in a channel?
- How are you pricing the product — as a substitute or value-added product?
- If you are relying on value to support the price, do you have your value strategy evidence in place?

If your business plan has not addressed the previous questions, at least in a preliminary context, then you cannot put forward a credible revenue equation. However, if you have done your marketing homework you are ready to create a monthly extrapolation of the price, quantity and resulting revenue expectations.

Staffing Assumptions

For most start-up companies I have worked with, direct staffing expenses represent at least 70% of the development stage expenses. This 70% factor usually decreases as a company matures into the operating stage. Within the context of this chapter, I include as direct staffing expense gross salaries, bonus (sign-on and performance), commissions, fully loaded benefits (medical, dental, workers' compensation, etc.) and employer taxes. Indirect costs tied to staffing probably represent all but 5% of the remaining portion. In this chapter I include as indirect costs recruiting, relocation, expenses generated by the staff (e.g. rent, phones, travel, subscriptions, dues, etc.) and outsourced functions (e.g. consultants, public relations, legal, accounting, payroll, etc,). Therefore, staffing decisions figure strongly in the burn rates the company will experience, as well as the level of control on specific projects and the organizational pain encountered when changes are required.

> *... staffing decisions are the keys to determining how effectively business plan execution steps are achieved.*

Even in fast economic times staffing up is a lot easier than staffing down. The implication is that extreme care must be taken to ensure the burn rate is sustainable.

Just as important as the high impact of staffing decisions on expenses, staffing decisions are the keys to determining how effectively business plan execution steps are realized. Therefore, the requirements of each staff member — talents, level, timing, and value to the company — must be thoroughly understood and clarified as part of the business planning process. Staffing issues are discussed in detail within Chapter Eight – "Intelligent Staffing."

Once the business model decisions are made (including the staffing and revenue assumptions), the expense components of the financial plan can be developed. The largest controllable factor in this phase is being realistic about the salary and associated acquisition cost of each employee. Much less controllable in recent times is the time horizon experienced to find and sign new employees. As a result the financial plan in many cases should reflect an extra one or two months (or more depending on the level of the position) for a full search. As you list the expense details for your staffing plan, use one-twelfth of the annual cost per monthly period (don't get cute and factor vacation and other paid time off separately). Spend the extra time required to ensure you have included realistic expense levels for all outsourced functions.

Financial Plan Mechanics

A basic profit and loss statement is a requirement of all financial plans. Unless you have a capital-intensive business, your company — like most other start-up companies — will not need to develop a formal balance sheet or a separate cash flow model as part of the initial financial plan. Capital equipment and other non-expense cash outlays can be listed directly below a profit and loss statement to create a combined profit and loss/cash flow statement.

> *Strive to keep the financial plan simple, but also responsive to rapid and easy modification of the assumptions.*

However, expectations of large receivable, inventory, equipment or payable balances would require special handling on a separate cash flow model to reflect the timing issues. And as the company starts to grow a separate cash flow statement and balance sheet become mandatory. During major growth periods the cash flow timing effects of increased receivables, assets and payables become significant issues for a company.

Strive to keep the financial plan simple, but also responsive to rapid and easy modification of the assumptions. Development of the plan is performed in reverse order to the eventual presentation; i.e. the quarterly summary is based on a roll-up of the detail worksheets, which contain the revenue and expense assumptions. However, the development begins with the detailed worksheets containing the revenue and expense assumptions. The detail sheets should have the following attributes:
- Ability to change pricing and volume assumptions quickly.
- Linkage of cost of sales to revenue (whether the cost of goods sold is a direct percentage of the revenue, or it inherently affects manufacturing or deployment headcount).

- Ability for quick adjustments of the level, timing and cost of the staffing headcount.
- Linkage of additional direct staffing expenses (e.g., bonus & taxes) and indirect staffing expenses (e.g., travel, phones & supplies) to the headcount. The expenses are usually linked as a percent for taxes & benefits and as a dollar per month, per employee, for other items such as travel and phones.
- Ability to consolidate expense items into the summary presentation categories (e.g., cost of sales, research & development, sales & marketing and general & administrative categories).
- Presentation capability for the occasion when a viewer is ready to dig deep into the detailed worksheets.
- A capital expenditure section (some capital expenditures such as personal computers should be directly linked to the headcount).
- Consistency with your historical accounting system in order to allow comparison of the financial plan to actual results.

Likewise the summary of the plan must also contain a few key attributes:
- A descriptive title including the company name, date and rounding conventions (most likely rounded in thousands of dollars).
- Previous quarters historical results if relevant.
- A column for each quarter and a total for the time horizon of the financial plan.
- Major categories (Sales, Cost of Goods Sold, Research & Development, Sales & Marketing, General & Administrative).
- Subtotals at the Gross and Operating Margin lines along with Margin Percentages.
- A Capital Expenditure summary line.
- Per Quarter and Cumulative Cash Burn totals.
- Don't cram too much on one page; the summary should be very easy to read, even if transferred to an alternative Word document or PowerPoint summary.

An example of a financial plan built on these principles is shown at the end of this chapter.

Industry Comparisons

Before you say, "We're finished," keep in mind that your plan will be held up against various yardsticks. Those who scrutinize your plan will also begin their comparison with a review of public companies in the same market space. You may anticipate this critical scrutiny by performing a review and studying the results in comparison to your own plan. Trending several quarters of these companies' profit and loss summary information — along with other measurements such as headcount, pricing trends, capital investment, and historical market capitalizations — will give you a good start. Note the product vs.

service revenue percentages and the gross margin percentages, as well as the relative proportions of the operating components (research & development, sales & marketing, general & administrative). If your plan is different from the public company averages, ask yourself why. If one public company is different from the rest, why exactly is it different? There may be legitimate reasons for these differences including the need to spend money developing the operational functions in advance of revenue growth. You must understand those differences and be able to link them to your business model, and therefore be able to defend your model. An example of an industry financial comparison is shown at the end of this chapter.

In addition to the above comparisons, you should review several other key factors related to your public competitor's financial structure. The following questions can elucidate these factors:

- What are the current trends in their revenue lines and market capitalization?
- When in their lifetimes did these companies experience geometric growth in their revenue lines?
- How have the operating cost percentages varied over their evolution cycle?
- How are the companies valued by the financial marketplace – as a multiple of revenues, as a multiple of profits?
- Why do some companies show a higher market multiple than the other competitors?
- Is there a *de facto* modified industry standard to the summary presentation format of the profit and loss data?

Knowing these answers by heart will give you better confidence in your financial plan, reassure you that you are on the right track, and help point you to more credible long-range projections.

Long-Range Projections

Are long-range projections of any value for a start-up company? For most start-ups my answer would be yes, definitely, but not as a realistic portrayal of the likely results of your company. No one really believes that you have found the magic crystal ball. You are also very likely to modify your market share accumulation and breakeven objectives based on future market dynamics. Nonetheless, long-range projections do have their value in answering some fundamental questions:

- When do you expect your company will really achieve a geometric growth in the top-line revenue?
- If revenue grows by a given factor, how much slower would operating expenses need to grow in order to achieve your eventual target percentages of revenue, and your targeted operating profit line?
- If profitability is reached only after your short-term financial planning horizon, what is the total cash burn required to achieve this milestone?

Remember, a potential investor will consider the market size and growth rate in order to gauge whether an excellent product is likely to be "sucked up" by the vacuum created in the marketplace. That investor will not consider unrealistic revenue numbers you project for the next three to four years. Remember also that investors themselves need to believe the long range potential is there – perhaps $100M annual revenue run rate in six years, and historically a run rate of $12M to $15M revenue per quarter is a common threshold for companies that are successful in executing an initial public offering (IPO). These ranges do change in conjunction with the current state of the financial marketplace.

> *No one really believes you have found the magic crystal ball.*

When you put together a long-range projection, keep it simple. Start with the summary presentation version of your short-term financial plan's full year total and project for three to four additional years on an annual basis. Again, instead of trying to come up with a perfect projection of the four to five-year horizon, learn how your company's financial behavior must change over time and how you can be prepared for those changes.

Conclusion

The creation of a sound, realistic financial plan for a start-up company depends significantly on the other components of the overall business plan. The financial plan serves as the feedback loop to test the validity of your business assumptions. Key goals in developing the financial plan include keeping the plan simple, yet flexible and responsive to rapid changes in the business assumptions. Benchmarking your financial plan to your competitor's actual results will give you added confidence in the validity of your business assumptions. Summary level long-range plans are also important for highlighting how the longer-term financial results of the company must be engineered.

Quicksilver Sample, Inc.
Sample One-Year Combined Loss & Cash Flow Plan
($000's)

All Information Flows From Detailed Plans
Depreciation and Receivable/Payable Timing Differences Ignored as Immaterial

Summary Line	Information Source	Q1 '01	Q2 '01	Q3 '01	Q4 '01	Total Year
Product Sales	Product Sales Plan	$ -	$ -	$ 25	$ 155	$ 180
Service Revenue	Service Revenue Plan	-	-	-	45	45
Total Revenue		-	-	25	200	225
Cost of Product Sales	Product Sales Plan	-	-	4	23	27
Cost of Service Revenue	Service Revenue Plan	-	-	-	23	23
Total Cost of Goods Sold		-	-	4	46	50
Gross Profit		-	-	21	154	176
Gross Profit %		-	-	85	77	78
Engineering	Engineering Expense Plan	86	183	174	180	623
Sales & Marketing	Sales & Mkt. Expense Plan	20	30	30	55	135
General & Admin	General & Admin. Expense Plan	15	15	29	32	91
Total Operating Expenses		121	228	233	267	849
Net Operating Loss		$ (121)	$ (228)	$ (212)	$ (113)	$ (674)
Capital Expenditures	Sum from All Dept's Expense Plans	22	8	15	6	51
Net Cash Flow - Burn		(143)	(236)	(227)	(119)	(725)
Cumulative Net Cash Flow - Burn		(143)	(379)	(606)	(725)	
Gross Cash Burn		(143)	(236)	(252)	(319)	(950)
Cumulative Gross Cash Burn		(143)	(379)	(631)	(950)	

Quicksilver Sample, Inc.
Sample Revenue Plan
($000's)

		Variables

Product Sales

Product			Q1 '01	Q2 '01	Q3 '01	Q4 '01	Total Year
Number One	Units		0	0	1	3	4
	Avg. Sales Price		$ 25.0	$ 25.0	$ 25.0	$ 45.0	$ 40.0
	Revenue		-	-	25	135	160
Number Two	Units		0	0	0	1	1
	Avg. Sales Price		$ 20.00	$ 20.00	$ 20.00	$ 20.00	$ 20.0
	Revenue		-	-	-	20	20
Number Three	Units		0	0	0	0	0
	Avg. Sales Price		$ 40.0	$ 40.0	$ 40.0	$ 40.0	$ -
	Revenue		-	-	-	-	-
Number Four	Units		0	0	0	0	0
	Avg. Sales Price					$	-
	Revenue		-	-	-	-	-
Total Revenue			$ -	$ -	$ 25	$ 155	$ 180

Commissions

Product	Commission Rate	Variable Base On					
Number One	10%	Sales Revenue	$ -	$ -	$ 3	$ 14	$ 16
Number Two	10%	Sales Revenue	-	-	-	2	2
Number Three	10%	Sales Revenue	-	-	-	-	-
Number Four	10%	Sales Revenue	-	-	-	-	-
Other Bonus			-		-	-	-
Total Commissions			$ -	$ -	$ 3	$ 16	$ 18

Cost of Goods Sold (COGS)

Product	Percent	Variable Base On					
Number One	15%	Sales Revenue	$ -	$ -	$ 4	$ 20	$ 24
Number Two	15%	Sales Revenue	-	-	-	3	3
Number Three	15%	Sales Revenue	-	-	-	-	-
Number Four	15%	Sales Revenue	-	-	-	-	-
Total COGS			$ -	$ -	$ 4	$ 23	$ 27

Quicksilver Sample, Inc.
Sample Revenue Plan
($000's)

Variables

Service Revenue

Product			Q1 '01	Q2 '01	Q3 '01	Q4 '01	Total Year
Implementation	Units		0	0	0	3	3
	Avg. Sales Price		$ 10.0	$ 10.0	$ 10.0	$ 10.0	$ 10.0
	Revenue		-	-	-	30	30
Training	Units		0	0	0	3	3
	Avg. Sales Price		$ 5.00	$ 5.00	$ 5.00	$ 5.00	$ 5.0
	Revenue		-	-	-	15	15
Support	Units		0	0	0	0	0
	Avg. Sales Price		$ 6.0	$ 6.0	$ 6.0	$ 6.0	$ -
	Revenue		-	-	-	-	-
Consulting	Units		0	0	0	0	0
	Avg. Sales Price					$	-
	Revenue		-	-	-	-	-
Total Revenue			$ -	$ -	$ -	$ 45	$ 45

Commissions

Product	Commission Rate	Variable Base On					
Implementation	10%	Sales Revenue	$ -	$ -	$ -	$ 3	$ 3
Training	10%	Sales Revenue	-	-	-	2	2
Support	10%	Sales Revenue	-	-	-	-	-
Consulting	10%	Sales Revenue	-	-	-	-	-
Other Bonus			-	-	-	-	-
Total Commissions			$ -	$ -	$ -	$ 5	$ 5

Cost of Goods Sold (COGS)

Product	Percent	Variable Base On					
Implementation	50%	Sales Revenue	$ -	$ -	$ -	$ 15	$ 15
Training	50%	Sales Revenue	-	-	-	8	8
Support	50%	Sales Revenue	-	-	-	-	-
Consulting	50%	Sales Revenue	-	-	-	-	-
Total COGS			$ -	$ -	$ -	$ 23	$ 23

Quicksilver Sample, Inc.
Sample Department Expense Plan
($000's)

Intervening Columns Hidden for Illustration

Engineering Department

Headcount Calculations

Position	Employee Name	Month Hired	Month Term'ed		Month 1	Month 2		Quarter 3	Quarter 4	Year End
CTO	John Tortori	1			1	1		1	1	1
Engineering Mgr.	Open	3			0	0		1	1	1
Sr. Engineer	Open	4			0	0		1	1	1
Sr. Engineer	Steve Marks	1	7		1	1		0	0	0
Sr. Engineer	Open	12			0	0		0	1	1
Staff Engineer	Open	8			0	0		1	1	1
Data Base Engineer	Open	5			0	0		1	1	1

| Total Headcount | | | | | 2 | 2 | | 5 | 6 | 6 |

Salary Calculations

Position	Employee Name	Annual Salary	Percent Increase	Month Increase Effective	Month 1	Month 2		Quarter 3	Quarter 4	Total Year
CTO	John Tortori	$ 90	40%	7	$ 8	$ 8		$ 32	$ 32	$ 108
Engineering Mgr.	Open	150	0%		-	-		38	38	125
Sr. Engineer	Open	100	0%		-	-		25	25	75
Sr. Engineer	Steve Marks	120	0%		10	10		10	-	70
Sr. Engineer	Open	100	0%		-	-		-	8	8
Staff Engineer	Open	80	0%		-	-		13	20	33
Data Base Engineer	Open	90	0%		-	-		23	23	60

| Total Salaries | | | | | $ 18 | $ 18 | | $ 140 | $ 145 | $ 480 |

Variables

34

Quicksilver Sample, Inc.
Sample Department Expense Plan
($000's)

Intervening Columns Hidden for Illustration

Engineering Department | Variables |

Department Expenses					Month		Quarter		Total Year
Name	Budget Department	Account	Factor	Factor Applies To	1	2	3	4	
Salaries	All	6110			$ 18	$ 18	$ 140	$ 145	$ 480
Bonus/Commission	Sales & Marketing	6111	Flows From Revenue Plan		-	-	-	-	-
Employer Taxes	All	6112	6.5%	Salaries	1	1	9	9	31
Medical & Dental	All	6120	4.2%	Salaries	1	1	6	6	20
Temporary Help	All	6130					-	-	-
Relocation	All	6150	0.0%	Salaries	-	-	-	-	-
Recruiting	All	6160	0.0%	Salaries	-	-	-	-	-
Contractors	All	6170					-	-	-
All Travel Related	All	6210	$ 0.50	Per Employee	1	1	8	8	26
Sales Materials	Sales & Marketing	6310					-	-	-
Graphic Design	Sales & Marketing	6320					-	-	-
P R/Advertising	Sales & Marketing	6330					-	-	-
Trade Shows	Sales & Marketing	6340					-	-	-
Conf. & Seminars	All	6350	$ 0.13	Per Employee	0	0	2	2	7
Patents/Trademarks	Engineering	6410					-	10	30
Product Testing	Engineering	6420					10	-	30
Rent	General & Admin.	6510					-	-	-
Office Relocation	General & Admin.	6511					-	-	-
Utilities	General & Admin.	6512	$ 0.05	Per Employee	-	-	-	-	-
Telephone & Fax	General & Admin.	6514	$ 0.15	Per Employee	-	-	-	-	-
Commercial Insurance	General & Admin.	6516					-	-	-
Repairs & Maint.	General & Admin.	6518	$ 0.05	Per Employee	-	-	-	-	-
Office/Shared Supplies	General & Admin.	6520	$ 0.08	Per Employee	-	-	-	-	-
Dept. Specific Supplies	General & Admin.	6522	$ 0.15	Per Employee	-	-	-	-	-
Printing	General & Admin.	6524					-	-	-
Dues, Sub., Books	General & Admin.	6530	$ 0.10	Per Employee	-	-	-	-	-
Postage	General & Admin.	6532					-	-	-
Legal, General	General & Admin.	6570					-	-	-
Employee Services	General & Admin.	6580	$ 0.05	Per Employee	-	-	-	-	-
Bank Expenses	General & Admin.	6582					-	-	-
Audit & Tax	General & Admin.	6584					-	-	-
Data Services	General & Admin.	6586					-	-	-
Depreciation	General & Admin.	6590			-	-	-	-	-
Property Tax	General & Admin.	6592					-	-	-
Total					$ 21	$ 21	$ 174	$ 180	$ 623
Total Personnel Percent					94	94	89	89	85

Quicksilver Sample Inc.
Sample Department Expense Plan
($000's)

Engineering Department

Capital Purchases

Name	Budget Department	Account	Factor	Factor Applies To	Month 1	Month 2	Quarter 3	Quarter 4	Total Year
New Employees	All		$ 1.20	Per New Employee	$ 2	$ -	$ -	$ 1	$ 7
General Office	General & Admin.						-	-	-
Engineering Equip.	Engineering					10	10	-	20
Management Systems	General & Admin.						-	-	-
Total					$ 2	$ 10	$ 10	$ 1	$ 27
Cumulative Capital Purchases					$ 2	$ 12	$ 26	$ 27	
Gross Dept. Cash Burn					23	31	184	182	
Cumulative Depot. Cash Burn					$ 23	$ 54	$ 469	$ 651	

Variables

36

Quicksilver Sample, Inc.
Sample Four-Year Combined Profit (Loss) & Cash Flow Plan
($000's)

All Information Flows From Detailed Plans
Depreciation and Receivable/Payable Timing Differences Ignored as Immaterial

Summary Line	Year 1	Year 2	Year 3	Year 4	Four Years	Year 1	Year 2	Year 3	Year 4	Four Years
								Percentage		
Product Sales	$ 180	$ 770	$ 4,300	$ 17,400	$ 22,650	80	75	72	70	71
Service Revenue	45	260	1,650	7,500	9,455	20	25	28	30	29
Total Revenue	225	1,030	5,950	24,900	32,105	100	100	100	100	100
Cost of Product Sales	27	116	645	2,610	3,398	12	11	11	10	11
Cost of Service Revenue	23	130	825	3,750	4,728	10	13	14	15	15
Total Cost of Goods Sold	50	246	1,470	6,360	8,125	22	24	25	26	25
Gross Profit	176	785	4,480	18,540	23,980	78	76	75	74	75
Gross Profit %	78	76	75	74	75					
Engineering	623	1,280	3,645	7,300	12,848	277	124	61	29	40
Sales & Marketing	135	560	4,150	8,040	12,885	60	54	70	32	40
General & Admin	91	360	1,266	3,150	4,867	40	35	21	13	15
Total Operating Expenses	849	2,200	9,061	18,490	30,600	378	214	152	74	95
						-	-	-	-	-
Net Operating Loss	$ (674)	$ (1,416)	$ (4,581)	$ 50	$ (6,620)	(300)	(137)	(77)	0	(21)
Capital Expenditures	51	360	940	2,100	3,451					
Net Cash Flow - Burn	(725)	(1,776)	(5,521)	(2,050)	(10,071)					
Cumulative Net Cash Burn	(725)	(2,500)	(8,021)	(10,071)						
Gross Cash Burn	(950)	(2,806)	(11,471)	(26,950)	(42,176)					
Cumulative Gross Cash Burn	(950)	(3,755)	(15,226)	(42,176)						

Sample Competitive Financial Comparison (Accrue, NetGenesis, WebTrends)

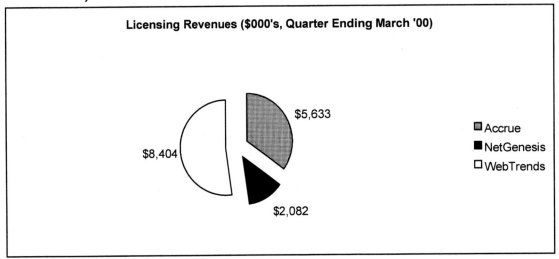

Licensing Revenues ($000's, Quarter Ending March '00)

$5,633

$8,404

$2,082

- Accrue
- NetGenesis
- WebTrends

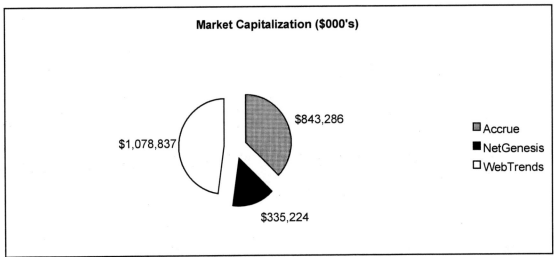

Market Capitalization ($000's)

$843,286

$1,078,837

$335,224

- Accrue
- NetGenesis
- WebTrends

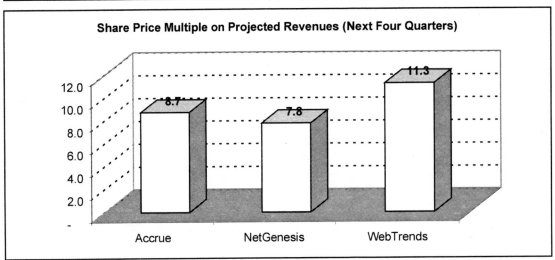

Share Price Multiple on Projected Revenues (Next Four Quarters)

Accrue 8.7	NetGenesis 7.8	WebTrends 11.3

Sample Competitive Financial Comparison (Accrue, NetGenesis, WebTrends)

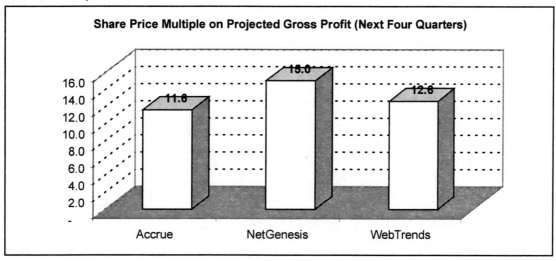

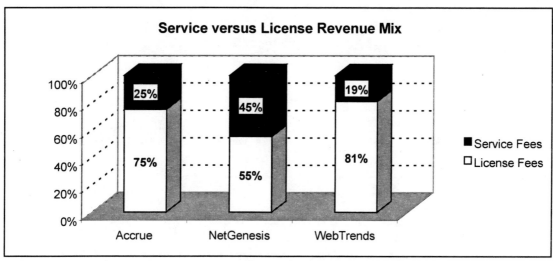

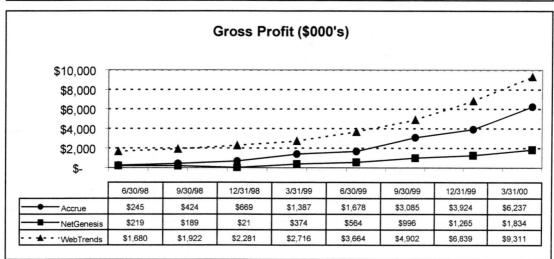

	6/30/98	9/30/98	12/31/98	3/31/99	6/30/99	9/30/99	12/31/99	3/31/00
Accrue	$245	$424	$669	$1,387	$1,678	$3,085	$3,924	$6,237
NetGenesis	$219	$189	$21	$374	$564	$996	$1,265	$1,834
WebTrends	$1,680	$1,922	$2,281	$2,716	$3,664	$4,902	$6,839	$9,311

Sample Competitive Financial Comparison (Accrue, NetGenesis, WebTrends)

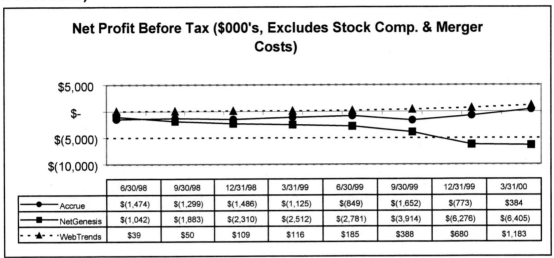

Net Profit Before Tax ($000's, Excludes Stock Comp. & Merger Costs)

	6/30/98	9/30/98	12/31/98	3/31/99	6/30/99	9/30/99	12/31/99	3/31/00
Accrue	$(1,474)	$(1,299)	$(1,486)	$(1,125)	$(849)	$(1,652)	$(773)	$384
NetGenesis	$(1,042)	$(1,883)	$(2,310)	$(2,512)	$(2,781)	$(3,914)	$(6,276)	$(6,405)
WebTrends	$39	$50	$109	$116	$185	$388	$680	$1,183

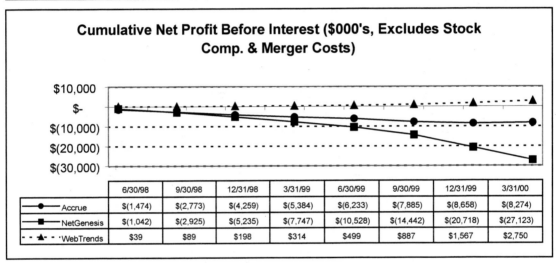

Cumulative Net Profit Before Interest ($000's, Excludes Stock Comp. & Merger Costs)

	6/30/98	9/30/98	12/31/98	3/31/99	6/30/99	9/30/99	12/31/99	3/31/00
Accrue	$(1,474)	$(2,773)	$(4,259)	$(5,384)	$(6,233)	$(7,885)	$(8,658)	$(8,274)
NetGenesis	$(1,042)	$(2,925)	$(5,235)	$(7,747)	$(10,528)	$(14,442)	$(20,718)	$(27,123)
WebTrends	$39	$89	$198	$314	$499	$887	$1,567	$2,750

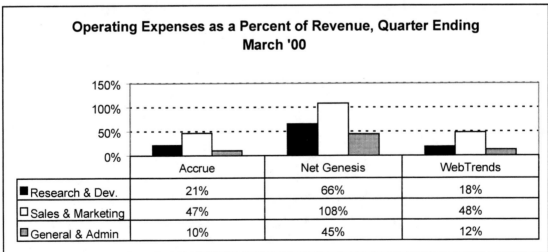

Operating Expenses as a Percent of Revenue, Quarter Ending March '00

	Accrue	Net Genesis	WebTrends
Research & Dev.	21%	66%	18%
Sales & Marketing	47%	108%	48%
General & Admin	10%	45%	12%

Capital Planning and Investor Targeting

Capital Planning

Capital planning—the meshing of investment resources to the needs of business development and expansion—is a continuous process. The capital plan is first developed in conjunction with the overall business plan and then regularly realigned as the business plan changes due to both internal and external events.

To illustrate this point, consider the product planning cycle. As products are developed, launched, extended and subsequently superseded, their life cycle is consistently monitored in respect to the marketplace. The product cannot be developed in isolation without considering the customer needs and competitive challenges. In fact, the prerequisite for development of a product is a meshing of what the customer wants and how to develop and deliver it to the marketplace. That meshing is reduced to the product specification under a cloak of secrecy. Studies, whether with development partners, focus groups or analysts, guide the development cycle. As the product is launched the push is on for reference customers and market awareness, thus gathering strategic evidence of the value delivered to customers. Subsequently, before demand decreases the next-generation product must be ready for the market.

Proactive capital planning moves through the same planning and execution stages, but instead of focusing on a product sold to customers, the product is the company, and it is sold to investors.

Successful companies place careful emphasis on reducing product development and introduction cycles, accelerating the "time to market" and "market penetration." Likewise, proper capital planning emphasizes reducing the closure cycle time for an investment round.

> *Proper capital planning moves through the same planning and execution stages, but instead of focusing on a product sold to customers, the product is the company, and it is sold to investors.*

Specifically, a primary focus is the reduction of time between the public push to engage potential investors and the "closure" (closure is defined as when the investors money is in your account). For example, consider the following hypothetical timelines:

Timeline A

Mar-01	Apr-01	May-01	Jun-01	Jul-01	Aug-01	Sep-01	Oct-01
Target	Negotiate		Closure		Cushion		

Timeline B

Jan-01	Feb-01	Mar-01	Apr-01	May-01	Jun-01	Jul-01	Aug-01	Sep-01	Oct-01
Target			Negotiate	Closure	Cushion				

Funding Timelines

Both hypothetical timelines result in a five month funding cycle. However, Timeline A creates a four month exposure to investor review of management execution and market conditions. In contrast, Timeline B creates only a two month exposure. Furthermore, funds are available two months earlier, leaving a longer cash cushion and therefore reducing the risk from a funding delay and allowing greater recovery/scale-down opportunities if funding is not obtained. A final benefit of Timeline B is high probability that the quality of the lead investor is greater, due to a higher emphasis on active targeting.

Reducing the exposure cycle is an outgrowth of three primary thrusts: development of a articulated, concise, executable business plan, active targeting of the potential lead investors prior to the public push, and proper planning for the due diligence process. A significant body of advice is available on business plan development, and a conceptual overview of the business plan was discussed in Chapter One – "Influencing Early-Stage Company Valuations," therefore, I will not cover its development comprehensively in this chapter. The planning of the due diligence process is the subject of Chapter Six – "Due Diligence Planning." The second half of this chapter is focused on the third thrust—the targeting of investors.

It is practical to avoid unwritten black out periods, specifically November 15th through January 5th of each year. These are tough times to draw attention to your company. The venture capitalist is most often occupied with the holiday season. Similarly, the month of August is a popular vacation month. Avoiding these periods and keeping a common sense glance at the calendar and current events does not guarantee certain success, but you should still consider these matters as you create your capital plan.

Assembling the Team

As in the process of executing an IPO, the company must assemble its internal and external team as part of the preparation for a funding round. Although the team is often lead by the CFO, the internal team also includes all key executives who must be available for face-to-face, first time lead investor discussions. The CEO leads investor discussions but all other members many be competent advocates of the company. If you are missing specific major functions on your management team, consider bringing in an advisor or consultant to assist during the critical meetings. The CFO serves as the clearinghouse of all requests and information flow; however, all key executives must treat investor inquiries as a priority during the active push. Confirm that all internal team members understand their roles, and resolve scheduling conflicts related to other major company initiatives and planned absences in advance.

External team members include your advisors, your corporate attorney, and your audit partner (if you have one, many seed round companies do not yet have an audit firm) and your references (potential customers, partners and personal). The external team members (except your corporate attorney) should not have to be directly involved during the targeting and negotiating phase; however, they should be prepared in advance for consultations, steering meetings and reference checks. As a part of the reference check, potential lead investors will likely want to see how stable your reference relationships are, and to look for validation supporting your strategic evidence.

How Much Do You Need and From Whom?

Your investment needs and timing are pegged to the milestones in your business plan and the realities of your financial plan. Acquiring too much money reduces your equity position but also reduces the risk of running out of money prior to achievement of crucial milestones, thus a risk-adverse posture. Conversely, raising too little money decreases the probability of milestone achievement and is therefore a risk-aggressive posture.

Sample Capital Plan Based on the Financial Plan Presented at the End of Chapter Two

Quarter	Milestones					Capital Needs Analysis			
	Technical/ Product	Customers/ Partners	Customer Segments	Management	Financial	Quarterly Net Cash Burn	Cumulative Net Cash Burn	Funds Raised	Cash Balance
Q1 '01	prototype	tested value proposition	customer entry segment targeted	CTO, CEO	seed funding	$ 143	$ 143	$ 600	$ 457
Q2 '01						236	379		221
Q3 '01	product available	first paying customers			1st Institutional money	227	606	1,000	994
Q4 '01				VP Mktg.		119	725		875
Q1 '02						250	975		625
Q2 '02		1st channel partner		VP Prof. Svc.	2nd institutional round	375	1,350	3,000	3,250
Q3 '02						500	1,850		2,750
Q4 '02				new CEO		650	2,500		2,100
Q1 '03		2nd channel partners			some corporate money	905	3,405	5,000	6,195
Q2 '03			2nd customer segment targeted			1,210	4,615		4,985
Q3 '03				full time CFO		1,550	6,165		3,435
Q4 '03	2nd product line introduced			VP Sales	quarterly loss peaks	1,856	8,021		1,579
Q1 '04					cash cushion money	1,220	9,241	5,000	5,359
Q2 '04						630	9,871		4,729
Q3 '04						300	10,171		4,429
Q4 '04					operational breakeven	(100)	10,071		4,529

Focusing your efforts too far towards either extreme will be viewed as poor management knowledge of the business plan. The total funding desired must also be matched to a realistic pre-money valuation of the company and the percentage of the company offered to the potential investors. You may find it helpful to review the Implicit Pre-Money Valuation table presented in the beginning of Chapter One – "Influencing Early-Stage Company Valuations."

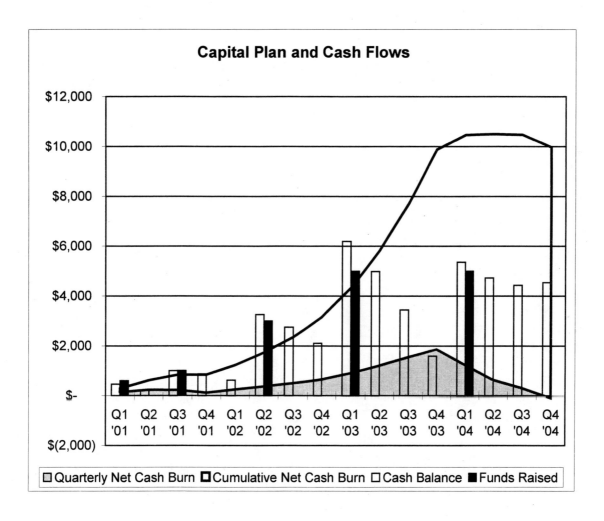

> *Total funding desired must also be matched to a realistic pre-money valuation of the company and the percentage of the company offered to the potential investors.*

Milestones must be clear, achievable and positively affect overall value. Many early-stage companies try to reach too many milestones, and set their milestones unrealistically. I therefore suggest you choose the three most important milestones for each funding stage and make them your primary focus. Be thorough and frank in calculating the resources required to meet each milestone and obtain both your investor and Board of Directors buy-in.

Investor Targeting

No attempt to chart the interactions of investment participants and company milestones fits perfectly across the range of all companies. However, an analysis of common norms, as shown in the following table, provides a framework for developing your company's specific capital plan. Charting the milestones of your business plan and the investment capital requirements of your financial plan will assist in both evaluating the timing and level of funding your company should target.

Ideally the seed round is used to lay the foundation for future investment rounds. Angels who want to participate in the seed round do so as a means to trade high risk for potentially high return; however, their follow-on potential is usually below the company's growing need of investment capital. Casual angels who are not investors on an ongoing regular basis move in and out of the market (in when the stock market looks rosy, out when the stock market looks bleak). Professional angels also move in and out of the market but are more likely to have stronger ties to follow on venture funds. Venture funds that want to participate in the seed round do so as an attempt to influence the eventual outcome, and as a means of risking a limited amount of their fund's assets to secure the ability to participate in future rounds. Higher quality seed round venture funds are able to "cherry pick" the most promising of the early-stage crop.

Considering the time an investment is locked within the average portfolio company versus the profit potential and risk, the mezzanine round is often the most profitable. Rights to participate at this stage are commonly secured in earlier investment rounds. Keep in mind most venture funds look for eventual liquidity within five years from the investment, and have an average fund life between eight and nine years. And although venture funds have historically been happy to achieve an average annual return of twenty to twenty-five percent, their hurdle rate can be much higher to compensate for the expected fallout within the overall investment portfolio. Also, as liquidity paths tighten and time frames increase it is very common for the milestones required for a specific funding round to be greater. This is exactly what happened in 2000 and 2001; as the "Internet Bubble" deflated, true customer validation became a key milestone for seed stage companies and breakeven became a key milestone for latter stage companies.

Convertible Notes Used for Seed Funding

Often angel investors will wish to structure the seed round through a convertible note or credit line. The note or credit line is convertible by the angel into equity at the first true preferred stock round, but at a discount from the price set for the preferred stock of that round. Alternatively, the note may be structured to convert at the full price of the next preferred financing round and include a warrant for twenty-five percent to one hundred percent of the note value. The discounted conversion price of the note, or the alternative warrant coverage, are methods to compensate the angel for taking a higher risk prior to the emergence of a stronger funding source. The size of the discount or warrant coverage is dependent upon the angel's assessment of the company, the current market and the negotiation process. An example of how to calculate warrant coverage is presented in Chapter Five – "Understanding Term Sheets."

One benefit of a convertible note in lieu of straight equity at the seed stage is that the valuation discussion is postponed or sidestepped at this time. If the note or credit line is convertible at a discount then the investor also is guaranteed an up tick in the value of his money at the next round, provided a round occurs. However, this guarantee to the up tick uses the founders' (and other common shareholders') equity percentage as source of the guarantee. Two other possible disadvantages are that the angel may not want to convert the note at the next equity round, and the angel may own the technology and other assets of the company if no follow on investor is found. All in all, the convertible note can be a good choice for seed stage companies. I have even seen boutique seed stage venture funds use the convertible note as the basic tool of their investment portfolio.

Target Lead Investors

The thrust of your investor targeting efforts should be concentrated on the potential lead investor. The lead investor sets the terms of the investment round—including the pre-money valuation—and holds the cards necessary for the completion of a successful funding round. In targeting lead investors don't just consider potential investors who have approached your company. You should actively target whom you need as if you were pursuing the ideal reference customer. Focus in on alignment of your key goals with the value a targeted lead investor brings. Ask yourself "If I had my choice of investment from many sources, why would my choice be the best source?" Potential investors who score highest on this question are commonly referred to as "smart money" or "golden money."

Investment Stages and Associated Attributes

Investment Stage	Common Lead Investors	Common Non-Lead Investors	Common Funding Range	Common Company Milestones Achieved Prior to the Funding Round
Seed	S, A, SA, BVC	A, F&F	< $1M	Concept & prototype, bus. plan w/ value proposition & mkt. segment identified, key technologist.
Early	SA, BVC, IVC, MVC	PRI, SA, BVC, CVC F&F	$2M to $10M	Beta testing or first customers, full mktg. & sales plan, most key mgmt.
Mid	IVC, MVC	PRI, BVC, IVC, CVC	$7.5M to $20M	Volume sales, customer segment leverage, alliances, all key mgmt., gross profits.
Mezzanine	MVC, PEG	PRI, BVC, IVC, CVC	> $15M	Multiple product lines, mkt. leadership position, operating profit.

A – Angel, BVC – Boutique Venture Capital Fund, CVC – Corporate Venture Capital Fund, F&F – Family and Friends, IVC – Intermediate Venture Capital Fund, MVC – Marquee Venture Capital Fund, PRI – Prior Round Investors, PEG – Private Equity Group, S – Self, SA – Super Angel

Investor Qualitative Descriptions – Positives, Negatives, Target Notes

Investor Type	Potential Positives	Potential Negatives	Target Notes
Angel – Accomplished individual, net worth > $2M.	Large numbers, some network potential, low risk from turndown, considers new mgmt. teams.	Limited additional value, no follow-on potential, limited network.	Through personal network for individuals, can approach some angel groups without introduction, may use convertible debt as investment vehicle.
Super Angel – Major successes accomplished, net worth >$50M.	Midas reputation, follow-on, network, low risk from turndown, considers new mgmt. teams.	Branded as "SA's" company, inactive but lock on Chairmanship.	Through personal network, may need to go through staff screen.
Boutique VC – Experience & track record varies widely, fund size <$100M.	Active involvement, niche knowledge, will consider new management teams.	Spotty experience, no proven lasting power.	Through personal network or from niche shows, events, & publicity.
Intermediate VC – Experience & track record has allowed multiple funds of increasing size, fund size $50M to $250M.	Reputation, follow on capacity, larger network, attraction of mgmt. candidates, customers & partners, imposes discipline, exit strategy support.	Mgmt. change imposed, higher risk from turndowns, tighter major decision controls.	Through personal network or from niche shows, events, & publicity.
Marquee VC – Known for successful investments, well-known partners & methods, >$500M.	Reputation, follow-on capacity, large network, attraction of mgmt. candidates, customers & partners, imposes discipline, exit strategy support.	Mgmt. Change imposed, higher risk from turndowns, tighter major decision controls.	Through personal network or from niche shows, events, & publicity.
Corporate VC – Successful corporation uses cash resources to directly fund companies with synergistic attributes.	Coattail effect, partnering, possible acquirer, often not active in company mgmt., synergistic focus as well as financial return, technology and market validation.	Block to other partners or customers, limits investment per accounting rules, longer sell cycle, may move in and out of funding market, may use funding to develop market and therefore fund competitors.	Often required to have Division VP argue your case to internal VC group, can sometimes be brought in by strong lead VC.
Private Equity Group – Funds pool focused on less risky capital-intensive industries, considers turnaround situations.	Appropriate if capital intensive or growth slowdown occurs, or if liquidity event pushed back.	Mgmt. Change imposed, tighter major decision controls, investment bank cost.	Often, but not always, approached through investment bank.

Potential investors who score low on this question are commonly referred to as "dumb money" or "green money." Also keep in mind that a qualified potential lead investor in an early-stage company should be able to bring 50% or more of the funding round.

> *... do not let your referral sources jump the gun and initiate contact before your all-out public push.*

In addition to identifying potential leads yourself, refer to your network, including your Board of Directors, your advisors and your trusted partners (attorneys, bankers, your audit partner, consultants). However, do not let your referral sources jump the gun and initiate contact before your all out public push. Finally, obtain agreement from your Board of Directors on your target list.

Research and Pre-Qualification

Once you have developed a target list, work steadily to research your leads, qualifying them every step of the way. Later, during the question and answer session of meetings and through follow-up correspondence, be sure to validate your qualification research and fill in the empty holes. Questions to ask include:

Referral Path
- Do you have a referral path to the lead investor's partner who is responsible for investments in your space?
- How strong is your referral path, can you find a stronger path?
- What reputation does the investor have - review press comments, talk to your referral source and extended team?

Funding
- What is their average and range of initial and follow-on investments?
- What is their valuation pain point for this stage of investment?
- How large is the fund, how much has been funded by their backers to date, how much is committed to investments to date?
- Where does their funding come from (i.e. is it a stable source)?

Decisions
- How well do we fit your profile, what portfolio companies are competitive, synergistic?
- What is the decision process?
- At what stage do they perform which aspects of the due diligence process?
- How do we measure up, what holes do you see (even if they have asked tough questions, summarize the results and ask if there are any additional issues)?

Post-Funding Relationship
- What do they expect from the company?
- How will they help the company, are they locally based?
- What is the common liquidity path; do they have relationships with specific potential next level funding sources?

The goal of the presentation process is to obtain term sheet proposals from two to three qualified lead investors. Do not confuse this overall goal with individual meeting goals (see Presentations below).

Non-Lead Investors

In general, finding top shelf fill-in investors to complete the round is easier after you have secured the lead investor. Usually the lead will want veto power over non-lead investors, ensuring they are value-added and not disruptive. The lead investor will also often have veteran fill-in investors to bring forward.

Therefore, avoid opportunism in encounters with potential non-lead investors despite the temptations. This is a good test of your business plan, style of presentation, and qualification list. Certainly avoid any promises of inclusion. If a potential investor persists, explain politely why you believe they are not qualified or suited as the lead, or if they are, when you will be ready to push the fund raising into high gear. Gracious, straightforward diplomacy is always the rule: you must never alienate a potential investor, even if you do not want the money. You might someday need to change your mind, and at the very least you do not want a sour reputation to precede the company.

A lead investor will want to know who else you are talking with, therefore be forthright and make it clear that no promises have been made—you will want the lead investor's input and agreement. Balance the need to show other investors enthusiasm with pragmatism and keeping a close hand. Explain why your potential non-lead investors add value.

Even with all of the above cautions, do not overlook the value possible from strategic non-lead investors. These could be members of your legal, banking, advisor and consultant network, or contacts they know.

Presentations

You will need to develop a number of presentations geared to the specific presentation format and time. A three minute, stage based introduction of your company requires a condensed presentation and leaves little time for question and answer. An hour-long meeting requires greater depth and you must be prepared to answer repeated tough questions. If you do not know the answers, say so, ask for more information, and get back to them with your answer as quickly as possible.

Regardless of the presentation format, every successful presentation answers the assessment questions outlined in the Early-Stage Company Valuation Model presented in Chapter One – "Influencing Early-Stage Company Valuation" and is organized within the following presentation guidelines:

- Understand the ground rules as far in advance as possible - who will be present, what do they want to know and within what time frame?
- Practice, practice, practice - test your weak spots and videotape yourself and other company representatives, hire a speaking coach. Practice in front of a friendly, but critical and knowledgeable audience. These exercises may seem odious but they will refine your presentation greatly and point out weaknesses in your style.
- In smaller, initial meetings with potential investors the most common mistakes are related to the completeness of your business model and customer validation of your value proposition. Make sure you have had someone asking you tough and critical questions before you meet the potential investor.
- Audience attention is key: engage them early on with the technology advantage and the value proposition, learn how to gauge the audience yourself and have someone on your team be responsible for taking solid notes and observing audience attention and response during the entire meeting. Review and understand criticisms raised after the presentation is over.
- After you present your value proposition and business model, support it with a logical flow through your entire business plan. Cleary distinguish your current position versus your milestones and their expected occurrence. Demonstrate the technology at the appropriate time.
- Make sure your entire executive team is present, especially at the first one-on-one meeting; rehearse your handoffs to show confidence and the smooth interaction of the management team.
- Focus on the goal of the meeting. Like any relationship sales process, the goal of the first meeting is not to obtain an instant term sheet or commitment. Find out what the next steps are—your goal is to qualify the investor and generate their interest in a follow-up meeting.
- Follow up on open items quickly—promise response within a realistic time frame and then deliver. Failure to deliver promised items on time is a red flag warning to potential investors on the management teams inability to execute.
- Do not put a book presentation on a PowerPoint slide show. Consider you audience; the most they can read from on one screen is about five bullets containing a total of twenty-five words. What you want to display are the points you will talk to, the five snippets you want them to remember when they leave. Use graphs and pictures as much as possible.
- Keep the total slide length matched to the length of your presentation time. Twenty slides in an hour give you three minutes per side. By the time you discuss a slide and answer questions you will probably need four to five minutes per slide

depending on the size of your audience. So do not take thirty-five slides into an hour presentation, or twenty slides into an eight-minute presentation.

- Keep the comprehensive studies, white papers, detailed financial plans, etc. as handouts for *qualified* prospective investors.

Conclusion

Capital planning is a natural outgrowth of reconciling your focused business plan milestones and the resource needs of your integrated financial plan. Through effective capital planning, you are able to match funding to milestone achievement and future growth resource needs, thus maximizing value and minimizing risks. Planning the funding cycle significantly reduces risk by targeting the best potential investors in your expanded network and reducing the time that management spends under the microscope. Use a litmus test to flush out the ideal lead investors. A valid litmus test requires effective research and qualification of potential lead investors before your public push for funding. Finally, use the planning time to assemble your team and hone your presentation, testing and re-testing the presentation on critical audiences.

Alternatives to Equity Financing

Other than organic growth, there are two main alternatives to equity financing to fuel your company's growth. Debt financing—which carries the obligation to pay back the funding at a future date—and development agreement funding, which delivers the payback to your development partner in the form of preferences and opportunities. The allure of both of these financing vehicles lies in the *potential* for a lower total cost of capital and reduced equity dilution, and therefore increased return on equity (remember equity is your and your investors investment).

However, both alternatives come at the price of increased risk. For debt, the risk is the ability to pay back the funds when due, and the ability to perform within agreed upon covenant restrictions. For development agreements, the risk is in the ability to nurture a value-added relationship with your development partner, while working within the tangible and intangible restrictions placed on your business by the development agreement.

An Overview of Debt

The first question a prospective professional lender asks is "How will I get my money back?" If you cannot provide the reasonable proof that answers this question, do not ask for a loan. The second question a lender asks is "How risky is the payback?" You must convince the lender the risk is minimal. A few reference points are worth mentioning. First, banks are required by federal regulations to maintain loan losses at approximately one percent or less of their total loan portfolio. Second, they are lending their depositors' money, depositors who expect to receive their money back. Third, banks are highly leveraged institutions and are required by federal regulations to maintain an increased capital base for high-risk loans, which reduces their ability to make additional loans. These factors leave little room for error.

Venture lenders often use a fresh investment from a recognized venture capital source that is several multiples higher than the proposed loan as a validation screen on whether a venture company is promising enough to be successful. In this case the venture lender is piggybacking on the venture funds technical and market due diligence and is also putting faith on the venture funds ability and desire to continue funding the company (i.e. the venture company is not mature enough to payback the funding without additional equity). The freshness of the equity investment also reduces the risk by giving the company breathing room to reach important milestones.

In general the "sweet spot" (average size) of debt financing to early-stage companies seems to be between $250K and $500K, while the common range is between $50K on the low end to $1M on the high end.

Even if you have proof positive answers to the payback and risk questions discussed above, you still may not obtain a loan. Why is this so? Most companies in the business of lending money act as if they had a large bank of individually controlled money faucets positioned behind a master money control valve. The master money valve controls the overall lending flow, while each lending category is individually opened and closed.

> *The first question a prospective lender asks is "How will I get my money back?" If you cannot provide the reasonable proof that answers this question, do not ask for a loan.*

The master money valve is turned on and off based upon the overall market economy. When the equity markets are tight due to a perception of unfavorable economic turbulence, debt markets also tighten up, even in the face of declining interest rates. The lender must focus on a triage of existing loans, and concurrently, increase their loan loss reserves for their existing portfolio. In addition, the lender believes the economic climate does not favor positive performance variances to plan from new loan candidates and therefore equates the perceived risk of new loans as higher.

Individual lending category money faucets are turned on and off due both to market segment conditions and specific lender issues. For example, if a lender feels that he is overexposed to real estate, or that a particular area of real estate is problematic, then he tightens real estate loan criteria. The same thought process is used for technology and specific areas of technology. I spoke with one venture lender in early 2001 who said that he was still looking for enterprise software and optical opportunities, but any software associated with the Internet, no matter how remote, would not be considered. Since lending and traditional banking are different departments with different mandates within a larger organization, don't expect a banking relationship to be translated into a funding relationship if the economy is slowing or the lender has soured on your company's space.

These comments are not meant as a snipe at banks and other venture lenders. From the lender's standpoint these actions represent prudent portfolio management, a desire to maintain diversification, and to limit exposure to problematic sectors. Lenders must act in their best overall financial interest by maintaining the proper balance between sales (loans and services) and expenses (loan losses and service costs).

Banks also provide numerous services other than lending. Although many of these services (e.g. foreign exchange, trade finance, private banking) are generally not immediate concerns for early-stage companies they will soon become important for successful companies. In addition, a savvy banker will be attuned to the venture community and market environment, allowing the banker to act as a source of potential investment leads and market validation. Therefore, establishing a solid banking relationship benefits the early-stage company even if no immediate lending relationship is desired or possible.

Loan Terms

Loan terms vary based on loan size, security and purpose. Common terms include the time period of the loan commitment (e.g. a one-year credit line), the maximum loan amount, the interest rate (which in my opinion is the least important loan term issue for a technology start-up), covenants (restrictions on the company's business and financial behavior and therefore an important issue for companies without significant operating experience), and loan-to-value percentages and warrant coverage. The warrant coverage rate is the primary upside reward potential used to compensate the lender for the increased risk of lending to an early-stage company. In general, you can expect the terms to be tied to the risk/reward profile of the lender and to the risk/reward elements of the specific loan. The greater the risk assumed, the higher the loan cost.

Formula Loans

Formula Loans are also known as working capital loans. A formula loan is a credit line computed on the balance of your company's liquid assets, usually trade receivables. Some formula loans will also include finished goods inventory. The quality of your receivable portfolio, both in terms of the underlying customers, their payment history and outlook; and potential problems in your product's performance are some of the factors that will affect the perceived risk. In addition to working within the credit line limit and your loan-to-value ratio, you will be required to back out any customer disputes, specific unqualified accounts as well as receivables overdue by a preset number of days. Individual customers may also be limited to a maximum cap.

Fixed Asset Financings

Fixed asset financing is often done via leasing. Leasing allows, among other things, the ability to split ownership elements. Generally, the lessor keeps the tax depreciation benefit, but transfers the property tax, maintenance and insurance burdens to the lessee. Key concerns for the lender include how "core" the assets are to your business, how transferable they are to other business, and their obsolescence rates—often equipment becomes technologically obsolete before it becomes functionally obsolete. For many start-up companies, fixed asset financing is not as attractive as it once was, simply due to the outsourcing of the manufacturing process and a greater focus on technology (e.g. software development). As you make this determination remember that workstations, servers, test equipment and furniture are also considered fixed assets.

Often an equipment or software provider has the ability to arrange financing for you in an attractive manner. For fixed assets acquired from a diverse vendor group, the equipment leasing process can be handled by a bank or a specialized venture lease firm. Specialized venture lease firms have financial criteria and expectations similar to specialized venture lenders (discussed below).

Non-Formula Loans

Non-formula loans represent credit based on your good faith capability to repay. Do not expect a significant non-formula loan unless you have a demonstrated "free cash flow" to support the repayment. Free cash flow is the remaining positive cash flow available after the reinvestment necessary to sustain your business. You can also expect a lower loan amount at a higher cost than a formula loan, but often you can bundle a small non-formula loan onto a larger formula loan.

Government Guaranteed Loans

Most government guaranteed loan programs are not geared to early-stage venture companies. During the fiscal year ended September 30th, 2001 only 172 of the 50,400 Small Business Administration (SBA) loans funded were for start-up companies (Silicon Valley Business Ink, November 23rd, 2001). You will note from the discussions in this chapter on venture lending that most venture lenders are compensated for the significantly higher risk of lending to a start-up company through warrants which allow participation in the upside success of the company, and not through a higher interest rate.

The warrant coverage model is not the historical structure of the SBA or similar state loan guarantee programs. These programs are structured to allow lenders to accept marginal loans by providing an insurance guarantee for a nominal increased interest rate (e.g. an additional three percent). By the time most venture-backed companies are generating free cash flow these government guaranteed loans program offer to guarantee loan values that are often below the expanded growth needs of the venture company.

The SBA 7A program will guarantee term loans (up to a seven-year term for working capital or a 25 year term for real estate and equipment) up to the maximum of $1M at 75% to 85% depending upon the loan size (www.sba.gov/financing). The California State Loan Guaranty Program offers to guaranty term loans (up to a seven-year term) and lines of credit (up to a one-year term) at the maximum of $350K (80% of the loan total if under $350K). The average of size of an SBA loan for the fiscal year ended September 30th, 2001 was $246K (Silicon Valley Business Ink, November 23rd, 2001). The initiation of a government guarantee occurs through the lending institution providing the base loan and therefore if you believe these programs are appropriate for your credit needs then you should target a participating financial institution.

Internal Bridge Loans

Internal bridges are loans received from your current investors. In essence the current investor trades some of the increased equity possible now for the hoped for tradeoff of obtaining a future higher valuation. Do not be confused—this is not an altruistic proposition, but a method of leveraging their current equity from prior investment rounds into a higher valuation.

> ... internal bridge loans are not conceived as a strategy, but rather as a fallback tactic employed as result of miscalculating the resources or time required to meet major milestones, or as a response to negative market shifts on valuation parameters.

To illustrate this point I note that venture funds write up or down their investment in your company based on the valuation set at a new equity funding round by an independent lead investor. Therefore, the venture fund may use this method to avoid a down or neutral next round valuation.

Specifically, internal bridge loans are not conceived as a strategy, but rather as a fallback tactic employed as result of miscalculating the resources or time required to meet major milestones, or as a response to negative market shifts on valuation parameters. Miscalculations can be the result of the failure to raise adequate funding on the prior round, a delay in business execution, or from unfavorable funding delays.

One basic bridge loan term the company will want is automatic conversion of the bridge loans, either upon some period of time at an agreed upon valuation or upon the successful closure of a new equity funding. New equity investors do not want their money to be used for the retirement of the bridge loan. Of course, current investors who are willing to participate in a bridge loan will not want to agree to the automatic conversion provisions. The compromise is often reached by setting a minimum equity funding size to force automatic conversion, and by establishing a liberal conversion valuation for a time lapsed conversion. Internal bridge loans often contain nominal interest rates plus warrant coverage. A standard warrant coverage range is from 15% to 30% percent or more. If new funding is not obtained within an agreed time frame, then the warrant percentage may increase at a predetermined rate (e.g. 2.5% per month).

External Bridge Loans

External bridge loans are possible only when you have a firm commitment from a respected venture capital funding source (i.e. the venture capitalist is the lender's source of repayment) and the venture capitalist needs 30 to 60 days to close a capital call on its limited partner investors. Thus you cannot expect to receive more than 30 to 60 days cash burn from the external bridge. The major concern of the lender is the ability of your company to close the funding round successfully. Often the best source of an external bridge loan, providing it matches your needs, is from an introduction provided by a new lead equity venture capital investor. Whenever the equity funding market tightens the external bridge lender can be on the losing end of a pulled term sheet, so naturally working on a strong relationship with a venture capital firm is a prerequisite for the external bridge lender.

Convertible Notes

Angle investors often use convertible notes in lieu of a straight equity investment. The use of convertible notes for this purpose was discussed in Chapter Three – "Capital Planning and Investor Targeting."

Lender Sources for Formula Loans and Non-Formula Loans

In Silicon Valley the banks known to have an appetite for technology lending include Silicon Valley Bank, Imperial Bank (now part of Comerica), and Venture Banking Group (a subsidiary of Greater Bay Bancorp). Generally banks are less aggressive, and therefore have lower warrant coverage and interest rate requirements than non-bank venture finance lenders. On the negative side, banks offer lower loan sizes and impose stricter covenants.

Covenants can be risky for young, immature technology companies because the company's ability to predict future results is limited. This limited predictability is especially true for the revenue portion of their cash flow forecast. Re-negotiation of broken restrictive covenants commonly results in additional compensation to the lender to reflect the increased risk.

In Silicon Valley the venture finance companies with an appetite for technology lending include Transamerica Venture Finance and Heller (now a subsidiary of GE Capital). Venture finance companies like to ride the coattails of sizeable fresh equity investment in your company by brand name venture capital firms. Like banks and venture capital companies they tend to work with companies exploiting the "fashionable" technology of the day, and they evaluate the company's prospects using the same judgmental factors a venture capitalist will use.

External Lender Mechanics

After you have done some fundamental homework to clarify how debt financing can properly fit into your capital plan, you are ready to start targeting appropriate lenders. Caveats standard to venture capital targeting apply equally well to debt financing:

- Target the correct debt financing firms by doing your research and networking.
- Solid introductions from your board, investors, advisors, and peers that have been built on prior transactions are much more powerful than cold introductions.
- The introduction and negotiation steps for obtaining a credit facility follow the relationship sales process for equity funding. The goal of the first meeting is to build interest in your company and advance to the next stage.
- A comparison of two to three proposals gives you the flexibility to evaluate alternatives and a stronger negotiation hand on details (do not expect to change the fundamentals of the underlying proposal).
- Be prepared with proper planning to execute quickly on the due diligence and document review processes. Have your legal talent lined up and primed.

Quicksilver Sample, Inc.
Loan Proposal Summary Analysis

Note: Items on summary that differ from or elaborate on the written proposal are based on verbal discussions.

	Institution	Bank A	Venture Lender A		Bank B
General	Loan Limit	$2,000K	$4,000K		$2,000K
	Financing Type	A/R Line	Combined Line		A/R Line
	Subfacilities	$200K Non-formula, $500K L/C capacity under the $1,800K A/R formula	$2,000K A/R Line	$2,000K Non-formula Line	None
	Maturity	One year	One year		One Year
	Non-renewal Notice Period	No stated period will be in loan documents	Sixty days		No stated period will be in loan documents
Costs	Minimum Interest	None	Not less than 8.5% rate and $7.5K per/mo.		None
	Prime Plus	1.25%	2.00%	3.50%	0.75%
	Origination Fees	$10K	$20K	$30K	$2K
	Warrant Type	Series C Preferred Stock at closing price	Series C Preferred Stock at closing price		Series C Preferred Stock at closing price
	Warrant Coverage	4% at Series C Preferred Stock Price	10,000 (2.5% at $4/share, 3.5% at $6/share)	40,000 (10% at $4/share, 14% at $6/share)	5% at Series C Preferred Stock Price
	Warrant Term	Seven Years	Seven Years		Five Years
	Est. App. & Doc. Fees	$5K	$6K	$6K	$4K
	Expected Renewal Costs	$10K, possibly warrants	$10K	$15K	Fee will probably be higher than first year since no new warrants are anticipated
Other Issues	Collateral	First with additional lien on intellectual assets	First with additional lien on intellectual assets		First with additional lien on intellectual assets
	Willing to Subordinate	No	No		No
	Borrowing Formula	80%	85%	N/A	70%
	Concentration Issues	30% per account, Company Z exception to 50%	None	N/A	25% per account, unspecified exception for Company Z
	Foreign Receivables Included	Preapproved for Company Y and X only	Yes	N/A	Yes on specific preapproval
	Disallowed accounts	Invoices over 90, accounts w/ 50% over 90, contra	Invoices over 90, accounts w/ 50% over 90, contra	N/A	Invoices over 90, accounts w/ 50% over 90, contra
	Covenants	Yes, no set correction period	None stated or expected		Yes, no set cure period, more restrictive than Bank A
	Reporting (days)	15 borrowing base and aging, 30 financials	10 borrowing base, 10 to 20 aging, 30 financials		20 borrowing base and aging, 30 financials
	Annual Clean-Up Required	No	No	No	Typically No
	Other Conditions	Requires $12M Series C Preferred Stock Closure by X/XX/XX, banking relationship with Bank A	None stated, Series C Closure expected as requirement for non-formula component		Requires $10M NEW money Series C Preferred Stock Closure by X/XX/XX
	Usable upon documentation for Contract Manufacturer Standby L/C	No	N/A	Yes	No
	Projected Availability of Funds After Internal Decision Date	30 to 45 days	30 to 60 days		30 to 45 days

Another Alternative - Development Agreements

The second primary funding alternative to equity funding is a development agreement. Targeting, approaching, and negotiating a development agreement parallels the process for debt and equity findings. You should start by determining how a development agreement benefits both companies:

- Does your technology provide a cost savings for the development partner?
- Does your technology allow the development partner to reach new markets or new customers within their existing market?
- Does the technology provide a significant value advantage for their customers?
- Does your technology lead to a powerful time-to-market advantage for the development partner?

Development funding agreements require significant advance consideration to understand the mutual objectives. Unlike debt and equity funding, the terms of a development agreement are more openly negotiable by both parties and often the negotiation directly involves several functional executives.

Execution issues embodied in the agreement should not be taken lightly. Your goal is to build a sustainable business, and the execution issues are the constraints that you are agreeing to impose upon yourself. I have seen a company benefit from a terrific license fee, but subsequently become essentially rudderless due to a combination of customer segment exclusivity and poor sales follow through from their development partner.

> *Unlike debt and equity funding, the terms of a development agreement are more openly negotiable by both parties and often the negotiation directly involves several functional executives.*

Furthermore, since the company was removed from direct customer interaction, it has not been able to build strategy evidence supporting its value proposition. The company could not leverage expertise into other customer segments. Adding further insult, the company's development partner now considers the development agreement a favorite whipping boy when ranting about company mistakes. This start-up company clearly has not translated the development agreement into a sustainable business.

Before you start discussions, develop your own internal negotiating strategy. Create and quantify the value proposition that you expect will best sell the development agreement. Then create your term sheet guide, listing all of the points that the development agreement should cover and filling in your opening position and "walk away" position for each point. Make sure to consider which points your target partner will want included and which points will be "must haves" versus potential giveaways.

Payments From the Development Partner

Payments can be structured in many forms. Commonly a mix of the following are incorporated into a development agreement:

- Development cost reimbursement
- Up front license fees
- Time or milestone based license fees
- Per unit royalties
- End customer revenue sharing

> *Be sure to compare the timing of development costs to the payment plan to ensure cash flow is adequate for delivery of the final product. If milestones trigger payments then you must ensure the milestones are realistic and based upon objective, not subjective, criteria.*

Be sure to compare the timing of development costs to the payment plan to ensure cash flow is adequate for delivery of the final product. If milestones trigger payments then you must ensure the milestones are realistic and based upon objective, not subjective, criteria. Also be sure the agreement contains a cure period for correcting missed milestones. Consider also the milestones your development partner should meet—perhaps the delivery of specifications or the number of units sold and the default penalties if payments are not made when due.

Exclusivity

Exclusivity is a primary issue. How "locked in" with the development partner will you become? How locked out of other opportunities? Try to keep the time, geographic, market, and market segment exclusivities to the minimum. Remember, if you engineer a successful partnership, each of you will want to continue when the agreement is up for renewal. However, even if the partnership does not help your company—you are still obligated by the exclusivity clauses in the agreement. Often whatever exclusivity you give up can be tied to minimum sales results from your development partner.

Development, Enhancement and Deployment Considerations

Are you maintaining your core focus by accepting the development agreement? Lack of solid focus has a long, well documented history as a primary cause of organizational failure. One reason failure occurs from the lack of focus is because the further you stray from your decided focus; the more difficult it becomes to demonstrate a core competency.

The contract should contain a process for agreeing on the selection of initial customers, including consideration of the customer's ability to get real value from the product and cultivate the appropriate environment for success. After the initial development, how will enhancements be prioritized? Strive to keep your input in the enhancement decision process, and just as importantly, to ensure all enhancements are driven by a broad customer set. Likewise, can a process be created where customers continually migrate to the current release?

Pricing Preferences

Granting pricing preferences should not be done lightly if your development partner will be reselling the end product on an ongoing basis. This caution stems from the knowledge that future reseller and distribution partners often insist on a Most Favored Nation (MFN) clause. The MFN clause requires you to sell to the partner at the best price given to any other customer. Working around MFN clauses requires a little finesse to make some condition of the sale—volume, preference time term, features, sales force commission and training requirements, support requirements, branding, co-marketing support, etc.—distinct and quantifiably different to support the price differential. Even if your development agreement does not contain a MFN clause, consider how you should structure the development agreement to avoid complications with future partners.

Competing Products

In the ideal agreement (from your perspective) you would bar your development partner from adopting or developing completing products. At minimum there should be a notice period and a consequence incorporated into the agreement triggered by the adoption or development of competing products.

Cancellation, Renewal and Jurisdiction Clauses

Determine whether you want a broad or narrow cancellation clause and what penalties should be imposed for the cancellation. Should renewals be automatic and for what term(s). Provide for *force majeure* issues (events out of your and your partners control). Generally you will want to keep your home county and state as jurisdiction for the settlement of any disputes. If your development partner insists on another jurisdiction then confirm with your attorney that the jurisdiction is free from adverse legal conditions.

Co-Marketing and Sales

What co-marketing and sales obligations are incorporated into the agreement? There are many issues that can be considered. Some of these are:

- Active salesman dedicated to your product.
- Salesman commission and training requirements.
- Space within trade show booths.
- Featuring in standard price lists.
- Special sales incentives for your development partner's sales force (do not underestimate the need for attention by the sales force).
- Product introduction and training at the development partner's sales conferences.
- Joint sales calls.
- Access to customer lists.
- Integration into your development partner's product planning process.

Customer Contact

> *On the other hand your development partner often fears the lack of control. Overcoming the development partner's fear can be difficult – you will need to demonstrate or engineer the reasons why the development partner wins by allowing you direct customer access.*

Ideally you will want the capability to approach and work with your development partner's customer set directly (if the product will be used within your development partner's operations, then you want access to their employees). Access is extremely important to gather strategic evidence supporting your value proposition. Likewise, do not underplay the importance of obtaining follow-on implementation, customization, training and support revenue as well as gathering intelligence on potential product enhancements. Opportunities may also present themselves for complimentary product sales.

On the other hand, your development partner often fears lack of control in this arrangement. Overcoming the partner's fear can be difficult—you will need to demonstrate or engineer the reasons why the development partner wins by allowing you direct customer access. If your efforts to gain direct access to the customer set fail, then determine how will you at least gain knowledge of who is in the user base and how you will be able to measure the value they receive.

Intellectual Property Rights

Who will own the intellectual property generated from the development agreement? The answer needs to be detailed distinctly in the agreement. Arguably the more you give up in intellectual property rights the higher other compensating factors will need to be in order for you to consider the agreement a win for your company. Perhaps some of the resulting intellectual property will not be central to your business model and can be transferred. Sometimes you may have to resort to an equity give-up to maintain the intellectual property rights. If you must resort to an equity give-up, cash investment is preferred over warrants (both will be factored into the total diluted outstanding share equivalents when your next equity financing price is set, therefore put the cash in your pocket now).

Evolution of the Development Agreement

While writing the above suggestions for forging a solid development agreement, I was struck by how similar the criteria are to an agreement for a reseller or other distribution partner. In fact, take away some of the initial product development questions and the expectations for development funding and you have the criteria for a reseller agreement. The point I want to make from this observation is for you to think through the question "How do I want the partnership to evolve after the product development?"

Conclusion

The two common external funding alternatives to equity are debt and joint development agreements. Debt is appropriate for companies with a strong fresh equity investment, established revenue stream, or marketable tangible assets. Matching the lender and debt structure to the situation involves reviewing your requirements and asset base. Target, engage and negotiate potential lenders with the same foresight, sales orientation and purpose that you would use for an equity round. In some special cases bridge financing is appropriate—internal bridges for sidestepping funding and milestone mismatches, and external bridges for a one to two months temporary hold over between a firm equity commitment and funding.

Development agreements are tailor made for situations when you do not have an established product, or you are extending a product into new market territories. Selecting an appropriate development partner, gaining their interest and negotiating an agreement that creates a long-term "win/win" situation is most often a process several months long. Carefully ask yourself, "How will the company leverage the agreement into a sustainable well-balanced business model?" Quick agreements do happen occasionally. However, in my experience, quick agreements have often failed to achieve the long-term goals.

Understanding Term Sheets

"Price is not everything!" Sound familiar? It should, as the often-quoted caveat is most likely part of the justification you rely on when positioning your company's product or service.

The caveat is just as applicable to understanding financing term sheets, the negotiated conditions used as the basis of understanding reached (but not absolute) prior to closing document development, performance of due diligence, and, one hopes, final funding. But before I charge off on explaining, "what is everything," please let me take a moment to cover a few fundamentals and definitions related to term sheets and equity funding.

> *The stock price is not an independent variable within a term sheet. Stock price is instead a dependent calculation resulting from dividing the pre-money valuation (what the lead investor determines your company is worth today) by the total pre existing common stock equivalent shares in the eyes of the lead investor.*

Opening Definitions

The stock price is not an independent variable within a term sheet. Stock price is instead a dependent calculation resulting from dividing the pre-money valuation (what the lead investor determines your company is worth today) by the total pre-existing equivalent common shares in the eyes of the lead investor (i.e. the actual outstanding shares plus other shares the investor believes should be included). Most factors, other than the structural terms of the deal that determine the pre-money valuation are discussed at length in Chapter One – "Influencing Early-Stage Company Valuations." This chapter explores the actual deal structural terms embodied in the term sheet, i.e. the "everything" beyond the price.

$$\text{Preferred Stock Price} = \frac{\text{Pre-Money Value}}{\text{Preexisting Equivalent Common Shares}}$$

Preferred Stock Price - A Dependent Calculation

Post-money valuation is simply the pre-money valuation plus funds invested in the current stock round. When comparing a prior round to the next round, it is the prior round's post-money valuation that is compared to the next round's pre-money valuation. An "up round" occurs when a new pre-money valuation exceeds the prior round's post-money valuation. A "down round" occurs when a new pre-money valuation is lower than the prior round's post-money valuation.

The majority of deal structural terms that influence the pre-money valuation, and therefore the stock price of the round, can be classed into two categories: dilutive terms and control terms. These structural terms will vary based upon current external market factors and the venture capital firm's internal practices. The best way to know what is in vogue or reasonable at any particular time is to obtain several (two to three) term sheets, listen to your independent counsel, and consult with your contacts, advisors and board directors. Term sheets that have several abusive dilutive and control structural terms are referred to as "dirty." Conversely, "clean" term sheets do not have abusive dilutive and control structural terms.

Inexperienced founders sometimes have trouble understanding why investors in early-stage companies should have any special dilutive preferences or control structural terms. The answer has two basic components:
1. These investors are primarily buying preferred stock, which is priced several times more than your common stock.
2. These investors are betting on *your* ability to execute the business plan.

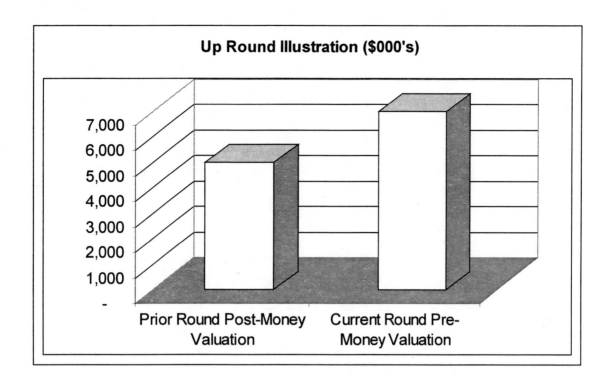

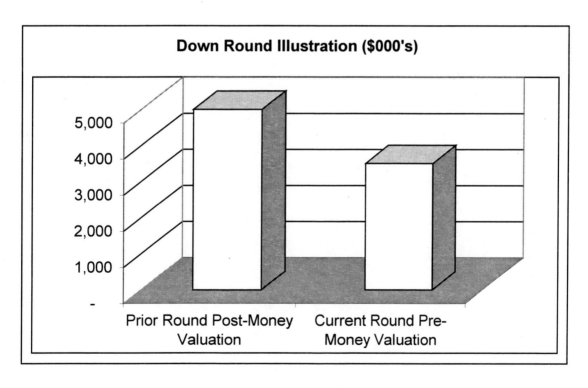

Dilutive Terms

The Option Pool

The size of the option pool included in the equivalent common shares outstanding directly affects the current financing round's stock price. The larger the options pool included, then the greater number of shares divided into the pre-money valuation, resulting in both a lower the per share stock price and a larger percentage of actual *outstanding* stock received by the new investor.

A reasonable rule of thumb is for the expected option grants covering the next twelve months (or the period expected before the next financing) to be included, and options required beyond this time frame to be excluded. Determining how many options are expected in the upcoming year is based upon the potential investors assumptions. You should walk through the assumptions with the investors to understand and influence their thought process, making sure the quantity correlates to your staffing plan.

Pre Investment Option Pool Dilution Effects on Voting Control

Current Outstanding Common Shares	3,000	3,000	3,000
Option Pool Required	300	600	900
New Preferred Shares Purchased	2,640	2,880	3,120
Pre-money Valuation	$ 7,500	$ 7,500	$ 7,500
New Preferred Funds Invested	$ 6,000	$ 6,000	$ 6,000

	10% Option Pool Requirement	20% Option Pool Requirement	30% Option Pool Requirement
Voting Control Post Round			
Current Outstanding Common Shares	53%	51%	49%
New Preferred Shares Purchased	47%	49%	51%
Price Per Preferred Share	$ 2.27	$ 2.08	$ 1.92

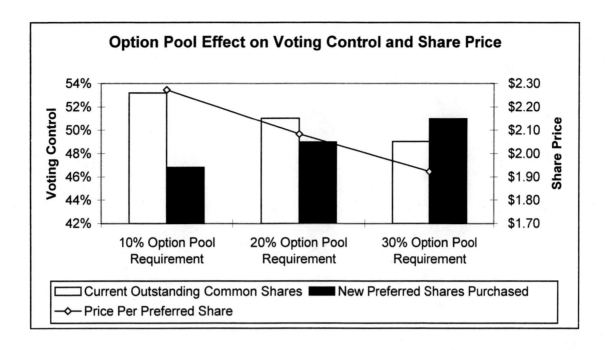

Most other dilutive terms do not have a direct impact on the current per-share stock price. They influence the investor's calculation of how much return they will obtain under various future stock rounds and liquidation events. I refer to these structural terms as post-dilutive events.

Accumulating Dividends

Accumulating dividends are dividends that automatically accrue on the preferred stock at the negotiated rate, regardless of company profits. However, they will not be paid until profits are achieved or a liquidation event occurs. They are therefore not guaranteed to the preferred shareholder but can still increase their share received from a liquidation event. Accumulating dividends come in and out of style and historically have been more common in financings originating outside of Silicon Valley.

Warrants

Warrants are the second most straightforward post-dilutive term. Warrants give the investor the right to purchase additional shares in the company at a predetermined strike price over a predetermined time period. The most common strike price is the current preferred stock round's share price, however some warrants are pegged at a penny per share. In the penny for share case the company receives essentially nothing for the warrant exercise and encounters additional accounting complexities. The most common warrant time period is from five to seven years. However, this can be negotiated within reason. Never accept warrants terms that are for the exercise of common stock shares, always insist on warrants for the current preferred stock class (accepting warrants for common stock shares will wreak complete havoc on your options pricing strategies). Most warrants also offer a "net exercise" capability that allows the holder to exercise the warrant for no additional out of pocket cost by trading in the appropriate number of the warrants. The appropriate number depends on the value of the stock at the time of exercise.

The final component of the warrant equation is how many warrants for each share of preferred stock bought, i.e. the warrant coverage rate. Warrant coverage is expressed as a percent. Fifteen percent warrant coverage represents the right to purchase fifteen additional shares for each one hundred shares originally purchased by the investor.

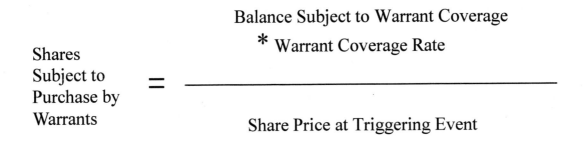

Warrant Coverage Formula

I opened the discussion on warrants by stating that warrants were the second most straightforward post-dilutive term and by now I am sure you are asking, "how can this be straightforward?" The answer lies in calculating the amount each shareholder will receive on a liquidation event, or the effect of a warrant exercise at the end of the term. Before one of these events, the warrant holder has no incentive to exercise the warrants and indeed will only exercise them upon the occurrence of a favorable liquidation event or if the company's value has increased and the warrants are due to expire. During a liquidation event, warrants are exercised coincident to the closure of the liquidation event.

Liquidation Preference

Liquidation preferences are the next step up the ladder of complexity. The basic premise of liquidation preferences is that the preferred shareholder is first in line for pay-outs from a liquidation event. Liquidation in this case means company is being acquired.

The complexities begin when an investor is allowed a multiple over and above their original investment (a preferred investor's original investment is always first in line), and if that investor is allowed to continue participation in additional pay-outs after this multiple is reached. Thus the liquidation preference is called either participating or non-participating.

Preferred shareholders with a liquidation preference and a participation clause have no incentive to convert their shares to common shares during a liquidation event. As successive preferred stock rounds occur liquidation preferences become layered on top of each other (e.g. after Series D's liquidation preference is satisfied then Series C's liquidation preference is satisfied, etc.). Sometimes earlier preferred stockholders are entitled to the liquidation preference *pro rata* (e.g. Series B and Series A on an equal percentage). The exact order is determined by negotiation between the shareholder classes.

Accumulating Dividends, Warrants and Liquidation Preferences Effects In a Sales Transaction (000's)

Example	Plain Vanilla	Accumulating Dividends	Warrants	Preference, No Participation	Preference and Participation
Common Shares	3,000	3,000	3,000	3,000	3,000
Preferred Shares	2,640	2,640	2,640	2,640	2,640
Preferred Funds Invested	$ 6,000	$ 6,000	$ 6,000	$ 6,000	$ 6,000
Accumulating Dividend Rate		10%			
Warrant Coverage Rate			25%		
Liquidation Preference Multiple				2	2
Participation				No	Yes

Company sold after two years for:	Percent of Sales Price to Preferred Shareholders				
	Plain Vanilla	Accumulating Dividends	Warrants	Preference, No Participation	Preference and Participation
$ 10,000	47%	53%	47%	100%	100%
$ 15,000	47%	51%	48%	80%	89%
$ 20,000	47%	50%	49%	60%	79%
$ 30,000	47%	49%	50%	47%	68%
$ 40,000	47%	48%	51%	47%	63%

Warrants are not exercised	Conversion to common is not forced

Accumulated dividends are paid first; remaining sales proceeds are divided by ownership percentage.

Warrants are exercised using a net exercise option.

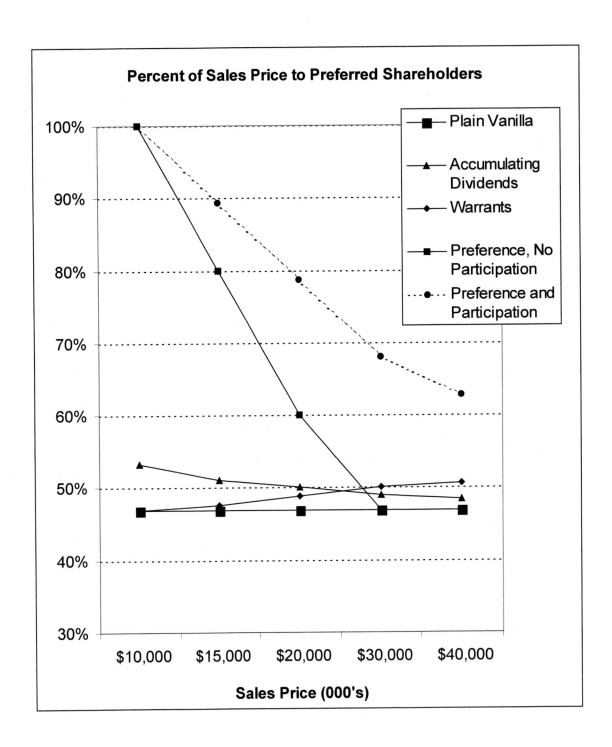

Redemption Rights

Redemption rights are commonly included in the term sheet. A standard clause may read, "At election of 50% of the Preferred Shareholders the Investors have the right to redeem their shares for original purchase price plus a rate of 10% per year." Redemption rights function as a mechanism to force the company's liquidation if progress has stalled and the potential investor believes this is the best way to recover some of their investment. If alternatives exist, e.g. a favorable merger or additional favorable financing, investors would probably not exercise their redemption rights provided their investment fund has not reached the liquidation stage.

Although Redemption Rights are standard, the triggering time frame before exercising the rights, and the percentage of shares that can be redeemed in one year are not. Therefore ensure that the triggering time frame is reasonably long (e.g. five years or longer) and the per year share percentage is less than 50% of the original shares.

Down Round Dilution (Antidilution)

One often encounters the request for protection from future down rounds. The most dilutive of the down round protections is called a "ratchet." A ratchet resets the price of a prior round's preferred stock to the lower price of future down round. For example if the Series A Preferred stock was priced at $4 per share, and the Series B Preferred stock is priced at $3 per share, the Series A price is effectively reset by the ratchet to $3 by modifying its conversion ratio (the number of common shares each share of preferred stock can be converted into) from 1:1 to 3:4.

> *The most dilutive of the down round protections is called a "ratchet." A ratchet resets the price of a prior round's preferred stock to the lower price of future down round.*

The ratchet and other down round dilution techniques therefore reallocate existing company ownership, reducing the ownership of shareholders without the protection and increasing the ownership of shareholders with the protection.

Ratchet Example (000's of Shares)

			Pre-Money Ownership
Common shares outstanding		7,000	70% Original
Preferred A shares outstanding		3,000	30% Original
Preferred A share price	$ 4.00		
Preferred A original conversion ratio		1:1	
Preferred B price	$ 3.00		
Preferred A revised conversion ratio		3:4	36% Revised

If you must agree to a ratchet clause, try to negotiate a time expiration into the clause (e.g. if a down round occurs over the next twelve months).

A weighted average protection clause is far less dilutive but a little harder to calculate. Weighted average protection reduces a prior round's stock price (again by modifying the conversion to common stock ratio) based on a weighted average of the outstanding shares. The weighted average can be either broad or narrow. A broad weighted average includes all common share equivalents while a narrow weighted average excludes specific groups of common share equivalents such as options, warrants or other convertibles. A broad weighted average is the least dilutive.

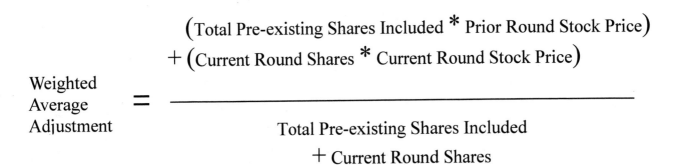

$$\text{Weighted Average Adjustment} = \frac{\left(\text{Total Pre-existing Shares Included} * \text{Prior Round Stock Price}\right) + \left(\text{Current Round Shares} * \text{Current Round Stock Price}\right)}{\text{Total Pre-existing Shares Included} + \text{Current Round Shares}}$$

Weighted Average Adjustment Formula

Under any down round scenario you should insist on specific events being carved out, or excluded, from triggering the dilution calculation. Common stock option grants, debt financing warrants, and merger and acquisition events are commonly carved out to avoid triggering the dilution calculation.

Weighted Average Adjustment Examples
(000's of Shares)

Common shares outstanding	7,000	7,000	7,000	7,000
Preferred A shares outstanding	3,000	3,000	3,000	3,000
Warrants outstanding	450	450	450	450
Options granted	754	754	754	754
Preferred A share price	$ 4.00	$ 4.00	$ 4.00	$ 4.00
Current round shares	4,000	2,000	4,000	6,000
Current round price	$ 3.00	$ 3.00	$ 3.50	$ 3.50
Weighted average adjusted price (used to modify the conversion ratio)				
Outstanding shares only	$ 3.71	$ 3.83	$ 3.86	$ 3.81 (narrow)
Outstanding shares & warrants	$ 3.72	$ 3.84	$ 3.86	3.82
Outstanding shares, warrants & options	$ 3.74	$ 3.85	$ 3.87	$ 3.83 (broad)
New equivalent common shares owned by Series A Preferred				
Outstanding shares only	3,231	3,130	3,111	3,148 (narrow)
Outstanding shares & warrants	3,223	3,126	3,108	3,143
Outstanding shares, warrants & options	3,211	3,118	3,102	3,137 (broad)

Control Terms

Election or Appointment of Directors

The single biggest control term that the company and the lead investor must agree upon is the apportionment of board directors and the Chairman of the Board. Be very cautious on granting director positions; getting rid of a director on a new financing can be very difficult. There is a practical limit to the size of your board, hoops to jump though if you want to expand it, and you want only active, value adding board members. The best advice I have is to keep the board small, as each future financing will drive increases in your board.

No-Shop Clauses

> *The single biggest control term that the company and the lead investor must agree upon is the apportionment of board directors and the Chairman of the Board.*

> *Always consider it a red flag when the potential lead investor allows a no-shop clause to expire.*

From the company's perspective, no-shop clauses that restrict your ability to negotiate with alternative funding sources are undesirable. However, the potential lead investor is very wary about being used to shop up the price or better the financing terms and wants to ensure a deal is not snagged out from under him or her after a preliminary agreement is reached. Therefore a no-shop clause will be required unless you truly do not need the potential investor's money. Do your best to keep the no-shop clause to a short time frame and narrowly focused on the specific type of financing. Try to keep debt, development agreement, and acquisition events excluded and, if you are in active negotiations on these alternatives, push for specific exclusions. Relying on the wording of the no-shop clause as applying to financings without bringing up the other financing possibilities is a weaker means of keeping the clause narrow, and may allow a legal challenge. Always consider it a red flag when the potential lead investor allows a no-shop clause to expire.

Conversion, Automatic Conversion

Generally each preferred stock investor will require the right to convert his or her shares at any time into common stock. Why would an investor and the company both want this right? The conversion right becomes a tradeoff between preferences an investor would receive in a liquidation (in this case a merger) versus participation in the upside at a favorable price. You will recall from the previous section on dilution that a preferred investor who has a liquidation preference coupled with uncapped participation has no incentive to convert his or her shares into common stock and the common shareholders will never participate equally in a favorable liquidation. On the other hand, a guarantee that the first money out goes to the preferred investors decreases their risk in achieving a positive investment return.

Conversion should be automatic if it is forced by either a majority of preferred stock vote or an IPO of a stated minimum. Most investors will naturally want to convert coincident to these events; however, the occasional rogue investor must be reigned in.

Restricted Actions

Several key decisions will also be subject to control clauses. Common examples of these key decisions are:
- Amendments to the rights, privileges, preferences or powers of a preferred stock class,
- Increases or decreases in the number of authorized shares (common or preferred),
- Creation of any stock class with equal or superior rights,
- Adverse amendments (in the eyes of a stock class) to the Articles of Incorporation or Bylaws,
- Merger or acquisition resulting in a change of control,
- Sale of substantially all of the company's assets,
- Repurchase of shares (except for unvested options),
- Declaring dividends,
- Increasing the authorized number of directors,
- Liquidation or dissolution of the company,
- Annual budgets,
- Major agreements,
- Key executive compensation and
- Increases or modifications to the option plan.

These actions are often both reserved as requiring a majority vote or super majority (as defined by the term sheet) of a single stock class and/or of all shareholders.

First Offer Rights

The investors will also want the right, on a pro rata basis, to purchase shares of any future financing except an IPO. It is also common for unexercised first offer rights to be transferable proportionally to other investors. Reasonable first offer rights should require the offer to be on the same terms and conditions as the proposed financing and should exclude employee option grants, public offerings, and acquisitions. However, keep the decision period to a minimum as this could delay future stock round closures. A workaround to overcome a long first offer rights period is to allow for two closings of the future stock round, the first one consisting of the bulk of new money and the second close consisting mainly of first offer rights exercises.

Founder Restrictions

There are three restrictions commonly placed on the founders. First is a co-sale arrangement in which, if a founder proposes to sell shares to a third party, the investors have the right to purchase those shares on a pro rata basis. This can pose problems in certain cases. At the minimum, exempt transfers to family for a reasonable percentage of your shares.

> *It may be advantageous to set up in advance a reverse vesting schedule, effective from the founding date of the company, to head off a request for reverse vesting from your first round investor.*

Second, the founders may be required to enter into a voting trust agreement that requires them to vote together on specific or all shareholders issues. Founders can often increase their overall bargaining position or reign in a wayward founder with this agreement.

The third restriction is the hold on the founders' employment via reverse vesting of their stock. This provision allows the company to repurchase unvested shares at cost. A common vesting schedule is a one-year cliff with additional pro rata vesting over the next 36 months. It may be advantageous to set up in advance a slightly more accelerated reverse vesting schedule, effective from the founding date of the company, to head off a request for reverse vesting from your first round investor.

Registration Rights

Demand rights, Form S-3 Registrations, Piggyback Registration rights and related items including associated expenses, transfer, and limitations on these rights should be reviewed with your counsel to ensure that the terms are reasonable and customary. These terms describe the means and mechanisms by which investors can demand or participate in public sales of your company's stock. An underwriter will also review these rights in detail during preparations to take the company public. If the underwriter does not like what it sees, it will require modifications, and most investors will agree due to the desire to complete a public offering.

Miscellaneous Terms and Components

A few other items such as the Closing Date, Information Rights, Key Man Insurance, Indemnification, Investment Expenses and the Capitalization Summary do not fit into the basic dilution and control classifications discussed above.

The closing date is the expected date when all closing documents (Bylaws, Stockholders' Rights Agreements and Stock Purchase Agreements) will be completed and agreed to by both sides, the due diligence process is complete and open items have been corrected or waived, and the money is available to change hands. Ideally the Closing Date is within sixty days, matched to the expiration of the No-shop Clause, and within your and the investors ability to perform. Reconciling these variables internally and with your potential lead investor is never easy.

Major investors will want rights to ongoing financial and other management reports from the company. A threshold should be placed on the ownership percentage required for Information Rights, and at a higher threshold you may be willing to grant Board Observation Rights. You will need to ascertain whether these requirements are within your capability. Many start-up companies overestimate their ability to deliver quality information in a timely fashion. I recommend that my clients consider carefully before accepting a proposal that is tighter then the Securities and Exchange Commission's (SEC) requirements for public companies.

Key Man Insurance, Indemnification and Investment Expense Reimbursement requirements should be reviewed for reasonableness. Get input on all of these from your attorney, and from your insurance broker for the Key Man Insurance.

For the term sheet you will need to provide a capitalization summary (table). Later, as part of the due diligence you will need to provide full details of each investor. A good capitalization summary provides both a summary by stock class and by major investor. An example of a capitalization summary is shown at the end of this chapter.

Conclusion

This chapter opened with the caveat that "Price is not everything!" Much of what is everything are the major deal structural terms contained in the term sheet. These major deal structural terms that surround the price can be broken into two major classifications:

- Dilutive Terms - Options pools, accumulating dividends, warrants, liquidation preferences, redemption rights, down round protections, and
- Control Terms - Board representation, no-shop clauses, conversion, other restrictive actions, first offer rights, founder restrictions and registration rights.

Each of these terms requires both a solid business and careful legal review. Your job is to ensure that you understand the business ramifications of each term, and to retain competent counsel for legal support and current climate benchmarking. Never, never, ever use the same counsel as your potential investor—this includes avoiding a reliance on a "Chinese wall" within a larger firm. You cannot afford to take the chance of receiving subjective advice.

Finally, remember that next round term sheets build in part on the deal structure of the previous round. Dirty terms on today's round will evolve into even dirtier terms on future rounds, and often require re-negotiation with prior round investors.

Quicksilver Sample, Inc.
Capitalization Summary
As of June, 2001
(000's)

Share Class		Undiluted					Diluted			
	Shares	Average Price	Total Investment	Conversion Ratio	Percent of Common Share Equivalents	Shares	Average Price	Total Investment	Conversion Ratio	Percent of Common Share Equivalents
Common	2,000	$ 0.20	$ 400	1	31.5%	2,000	$ 0.20	$ 400	1	24.0%
Preferred A	1,000	2.00	2,000	1	15.8%	1,000	2.00	2,000	1	12.0%
Preferred B	1,500	3.00	4,500	1	23.6%	1,500	3.00	4,500	1	18.0%
Preferred C	1,847	3.50	6,465	1	29.1%	1,847	3.50	6,465	1	22.2%
Granted Options						563	0.95		1	6.8%
Ungranted Options						437			1	5.2%
Allowance for Option Pool Increase						400			1	4.8%
Convertible Notes						250	4.00		1	3.0%
Warrants (Preferred C)						327	3.50		1	3.9%
Totals	6,347	$ 2.11	$ 13,365		100.0%	8,324		$13,365		100.0%

Shareholder Group		Undiluted					Diluted			
	Shares	Average Price	Total Investment	Conversion Ratio	Percent of Common Share Equivalents	Shares	Average Price	Total Investment	Conversion Ratio	Percent of Common Share Equivalents
Founders	2,000	$ 0.20	$ 400	1	31.5%	2,000	$ 0.20	$ 400	1	24.0%
Angel Investors	1,000	2.00	2,000	1	15.8%	1,000	2.00	2,000	1	12.0%
Venture A Fund	2,008	3.13	6,278	1	31.6%	2,008	3.13	6,278	1	24.1%
Venture B Fund	1,339	3.50	4,687	1	21.1%	1,339	3.50	4,687	1	16.1%
Current & Future Employees						1,400			1	16.8%
Convertible Debt Fund Z						300	3.92		1	3.6%
Venture A Fund						76	3.50		1	0.9%
Venture B Fund						201	3.50		1	2.4%
Totals	6,347	$ 2.11	$ 13,365		100.0%	8,324		$13,365		100.0%

Undiluted Ownership by Stock Class

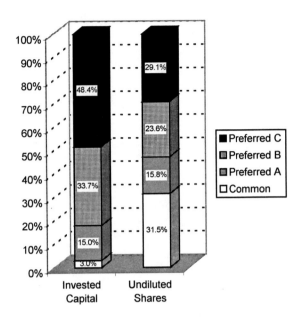

Undiluted Ownership by Investor

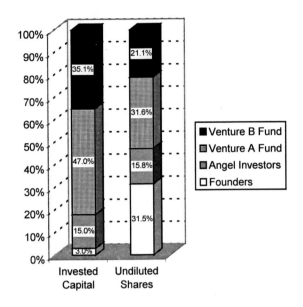

Diluted Ownership by Stock Class

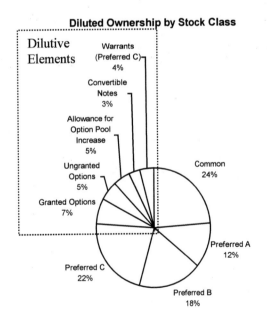

Diluted Ownership by Investor

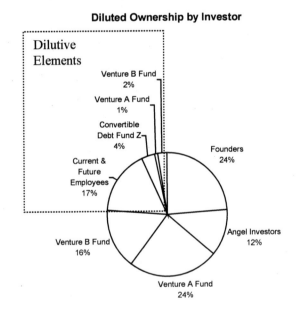

Quicksilver Sample Inc.
Capitalization Summary

Due Diligence Planning

The Purpose of Due Diligence Planning

What does an investor, lender or buyer want to know and how do you provide that knowledge?

Due diligence is the process whereby a prospective investor, lender or buyer (for convenience I will refer to all of these as the investor) reviews the risks associated with a company. The review is based upon information presented by the company, validated directly and through external sources, as the investor deems necessary. The outcome of the process is the decision that the risks associated with the contemplated transaction are known and prudent, or that they are not known or prudent. A positive decision outcome may help lead to a successful transaction close while a negative decision outcome prevents the closure.

The validation steps of a thorough due diligence review include the "tire kicking," or person to person follow up on references, facilities, customers, partners and suppliers. When I have participated on buyer side due diligence teams, the team reviewed the entire business of the targeted company in detail. We reconstructed forward-looking revenue and expense plans from on-site observations. We reviewed the manufacturing equipment for maintenance, throughput and yields. We talked to suppliers and customers, reviewed the contracts and historical interactions. Often target companies were unprepared for this level of face-to-face inspection. They also forgot to consider the reference checking aspects inherent in due diligence, and therefore found themselves wasting time collecting and priming their references during the due diligence process.

Another desired outcome of due diligence planning is the avoidance of surprises, thus lowering the buyer's risk assessment. Surprises such as "Where is the signed contract?" or "We do not have Confidentiality and Invention Assignment Agreements for several key employees?" should be eliminated at the start. Time spent closing loose ends during the due diligence process also distracts from the priorities of business execution and expediting the transaction closing documents.

> *But if you do have dirty laundry when the due diligence strikes – then admit it, address the risk posed by the dirty laundry, and lay out your corrective action plan. An investor will not put up with false, misleading or incomplete statements.*

But if you do have dirty laundry when the due diligence strikes, then admit it, address the risk posed by the dirty laundry, and lay out your corrective action plan. An investor will not put up with false, misleading or incomplete statements. Furthermore, all transaction-closing documents contain a management representation that all known and relevant facts have been fully and completely disclosed.

The majority of the company information that the investor requires, as a basis for formulating his or her risk decision and validation plan, is in paper and electronic files. Proper due diligence planning therefore also relies heavily on the organized collection of detailed information before the signing of a term sheet—not only does management appear active and prepared in this case but management also shortens the time frame in which business plan execution problems can derail the transaction.

Due Diligence Pyramid

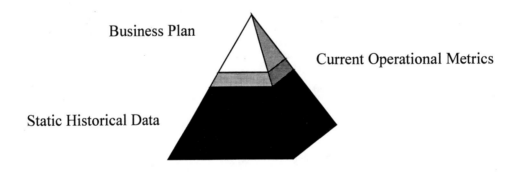

I believe it is very useful to organize supporting paper and electronic documents into three categories, which can be viewed as a partially buried pyramid. The top, most visible layer of the pyramid contains your business plan, associated sub-plans and references that are directly related to your funding efforts. This layer presents the forward-looking perspective of your company. The brighter the top layer shines the more initial interest you will have from potential investors. The middle layer is the thinnest layer and contains current operational metrics that you need to provide "as of" the start of the due diligence process. At the base of the pyramid, the part that is often buried and not easily viewed, is the significant majority of documents that detail the company's static historical record. Like the foundation of any structure, hidden cracks, holes and rot can collapse the pyramid. The following sections of this chapter address the content and planning tips related to these three pyramid layers.

Business Plan

Presenting a solid business plan was likely a major factor in the potential investor's decision process, a factor that encouraged the investor to extend a term sheet and start formal due diligence. However, during the due diligence process the potential investor will take a second, expanded look at validating the business plan. Questions asked at this stage may include:

- Is your market size truly as big as you estimated?
- How big a threat are your competitors?
- Is your distribution plan appropriate?
- Is your technological roadmap realistic?

Therefore, make sure your business plan is complete and you have valid external sources supporting your comparative data. The following items help make up a complete business plan. You may also want to review the visual diagram of the business plan shown in Chapter One – "Influencing Early-Stage Company Valuations."

A. Environmental Analysis
- Market, market segment & customer segment analysis
- Competitors list

B. Conceptual Models
- Business model
- Value proposition

C. Execution Plans
- Technology roadmap
- Capital plan
- Product development & engineering project plans
- Key customer target list
- Segment leveraging models
- Distribution plan
- PR, tradeshow & advertising plan
- Manufacturing plan
- Ranked customers and suppliers
- Organization chart
- Capitalization summary table, fully diluted—grouped both by shareholder class and by major shareholders

- Financial plan

D. Other
- Resumes & bios for key employees, directors, advisors
- References—customers, suppliers, partners, advisors, personal

Current Operational Metrics

The middle layer of the due diligence pyramid provides current metrics that reflect the state of your business. The potential investor uses this information to understand current business trends and issues. Some of the questions asked include:
- Is there an increase in returns?
- How much inventory is obsolete or in rework?
- What open sales and supply commitments does the company have?

These metrics cannot always be created before the start of the due diligence period, therefore you should make sure you have the operational capability to deliver them quickly. I observe that responsible companies prepare most of these metrics on a periodic or continual basis and therefore should be able to use a recent period end or generate them quickly. Other items, for instance a complete employee list with name, title, salary, bonus, options and other contractual agreements is probably not regularly prepared. In such cases it is worthwhile to prepare the list in advance, subsequently adding a quick update, or to break the list into definable components. The following current status documents are commonly requested by an investor:

- Employee lists - name, title, salary, bonus, options, other contractual agreements
- Most recent payroll
- Open employee requisitions and offers, position, proposed option grants
- Current ranked customer lists
- Open returns authorizations
- Open aged accounts receivable and accounts payable
- Open sales (backlog) and purchase commitments, significant related issues
- Current ranked vendor lists
- Current inventory, by product, by stage, by status
- Legal and audit comfort letters
- Equipment listing, owned and leased along with highlights of major changes
- Complete details supporting the capitalization summary—shareholder or option holder address, stock class, number of shares, phone number, contact name and stock/option grant reference numbers

Static Historical Records

The largest layer of the pyramid, the base, contains the documents that reflect your company's static historical record. As such, each document type should have a permanent owner within your organization. The owner should be cognizant and capable of his or her responsibility to keep accurate and complete files. When contacted in advance of funding negotiations, the owner should be able to provide due diligence copies to one control point within the organization, and subsequently to provide updated documents as they are executed. However, gathering the documents is not enough; the documents need to be reviewed for non-compliance, time to renewal and other open issues. Clean up these open issues before the due diligence starts. The following list is organized by topical area.

A. **Employment (for all employees unless indicated otherwise)**
- Unilateral Nondisclosure Agreements (NDA's) from all candidates
- Employment agreements
- Confidentiality and Invention Assignment Agreements
- Separation documents for all separated employees including any past, current, or pending disputes or related legal actions
- Employee plans including insurance, personnel policies, and 401K arrangements
- Option agreements
- Master option plan(s) and all amendments
- Employee loans

B. **Prior Financing Documents**
- Term sheets
- Definitive Stock Purchase Agreements
- Stockholders' Rights Agreements
- Bank credit line or debt agreements

C. **Corporate Organization**
- Articles of Incorporation & Bylaws plus all amendments
- "Good Standing" certificates
- Board of Directors meeting minutes, actions by written consent
- States & countries authorized to do business
- All office locations & subsidiaries (organizational documents)
- Founders' agreement, voting trusts
- Partnership or joint venture agreements
- Minority investments

D. **Marketing & Sales, Purchasing & Manufacturing**
- Bilateral and Unilateral Nondisclosure Agreements (NDA's)
- Sales & distribution contracts

- Purchasing & manufacturing contracts
- Contract term sheets for pending contracts
- License & royalty agreements
- Press releases
- Return, warranty & guarantee policies
- Training, service & support programs
- Market, product or other studies & research (internal, contracted & third party)
- Sales brochures and catalogs
- Current and historical price lists
- Details on all alpha & beta product tests and results
- Details on any third party testing of the product

E. Financial, Tax & Insurance

- Audited financial statements & internal financial statements, management letters
- Accounting policies and all major changes
- All leases and subleases
- Insider or shareholder transactions
- Income tax returns for all open years
- Inter-company and other tax agreements
- Insurance polices & claims history
- Workers compensation & claims history

F. Intellectual Property, Legal, Government

- Patent, trade secret, copyright & trademark filings, their status and any related issues
- Past, present or threatened litigation or infringement issues
- Notice by any contract party of noncompliance or non-renewal
- Government permits and licenses
- OSHA, FCC or other government agency compliance and regulation issues
- Environmental discharge issues
- Details on hazardous materials used, stored, transported or manufactured by the company, or by any other company in the company's locations
- Government orders or judgments whether open, closed or pending
- Security filings (UCC) for equipment (against or on behalf of the company)

I strongly advise my clients to keep a complete file copy of all due diligence materials presented to a potential investor with notes on whom they were sent to and on what date. This allows for additional copies of sections to be sent to the investor's counsel or accountants. It also helps the quick resolution of questions and expedites the completion of all exceptions to the Management's Representations and Warranties section of the closing documents. Finally, in the unlikely event that a post closing issue related to full disclosure occurs, the company has preserved the ability to respond properly.

> *... keep a complete file copy of all due diligence materials presented to a potential investor with notes on whom they were sent to and on what date.*

Conclusion

The purpose of due diligence planning is to shorten the funding cycle and increase the probability of closing the transaction. Management teams that have reviewed the issues in order to eliminate surprises and open items, align their references, and assemble a standard due diligence package appear prepared and responsible. Furthermore, during the due diligence period the management team can concentrate on business execution and closing document completion— reducing the chance of derailment—thereby decreasing the length of the investors' inspection window.

Twenty-One Common Myths About Funding

1. A signed term sheet is a firm commitment. *Due diligence and continued execution after the term sheet is signed are still major requirements. Potential investors can also be spooked by external market developments that change the valuation parameters.*

2. All potential investors and customers agree and have the right advice. *A few are just plain wrong; others may have different agendas that do not fit well with your company. Obtain several opinions and then formulate the best answer.*

3. All corporate venture groups have the same primary motivation (internal measurement criteria). *Some are driven by financial returns only, others primarily by market synergy. Most, but by no means all, have some element of both.*

4. No venture money is available. *Compelling companies with well articulated business plans that are properly shopped can get funded in almost every environment.*

5. All venture investors are out to get you. *Absolutes are rarely true; most venture investors believe that a "win/win" situation gives them the best possibility of higher returns.*

6. All venture investors are your best friend. *See 5.*

7. Potential investors are okay with you saying you will figure out how to use their money after you have it. *It is what you do with their money that matters most; everything else is just the appetizer.*

8. You do not need money. *You always need money, the best source and how much you can deploy effectively are the questions.*

9. A marquee investor or customer is all we need to be successful. *Obtaining one is a great milestone, but this is not a goal and you will need the investor's or customer's continued strong support.*

10. Focus means we will trade away a significant portion of our company's potential. *Focus is the path to start realizing your potential.*

11. If they do not get my message then they are stupid. *Maybe with one or two this is the case, but when more than two do not get the message, the odds are against you.*

12. Building a company and raising money is easy. *If building a company was easy, everyone would do it and be successful. Raising money often takes at least twice as long as you think and is almost always harder than it looks.*

13. How large a percentage of the company the founders retain is the most important thing. *What maters is the total value of your percentage. A smaller slice of a larger pie is worth a lot more than a large slice of nothing.*

14. Most successful companies obtain investor liquidity through an IPO. *Most successful companies achieve investor liquidity through being acquired. Although final valuations may be higher in an IPO, owners often can do very well and even better through an acquisition. Time to money, liquidity of the acquiring company's stock and additional interim dilution from future preferred stock rounds are some of the factors to consider.*

15. The right technology is all we need to raise money and be successful. *The world is full of bright technical ideas that have no value to the marketplace and management teams that cannot open a paper bag. Market size is an important determinant of the total value possible. The management team must be built on a core understanding of the technology's use in the marketplace, be coachable and willing to step aside when appropriate.*

16. A compelling business model is not a requirement for early-stage companies. *If you cannot show how you will increase shareholder value, why would a rationale person want to invest money?*

17. We already know what the customers want so we do not need to talk to them before the product is completed. *What? Need I say more?*

18. If you are turned down by a potential investor then never talk to them again. *If you obtained the reasons for their initial disinterest and have corrected them, then ask to pitch again. The first investor pitch is almost always a disaster, companies who obtain their trial by fire through multiple sessions with experienced advisors and non confrontational discussions with investor groups*

are able to work out many of the not so obvious bugs before the present to the potential investor with the "golden" money.

19.   A venture investor will never walk away if they have already invested money in your company. *A rationale person will not throw good money after bad. Poor company performance and shifts in the market dynamics are only two of the reasons why an investor would decline to invest more money.*

20.   Founders need to show a financial plan which ramps up to over $100M in revenue in 4 years to obtain venture capital interest. *Show me a financial plan without a fast growing market and explain to me how this revenue ramp occurs. Show me a financial plan without high sustainable margins and convince me the company is creating significant value. And how much capital investment do you need to obtain the plan? These factors, along with a convincing argument that execution is achievable, must all be present. All serious potential investors will create their own internal financial projection.*

21.   Obtaining funding is the goal. *Building a sustainable high growth company is the goal; obtaining funding is achieving a milestone on the path to the goal.*

Section Two

Early-Stage Financial Execution

Intelligent Staffing

I remember that as a youngster I stayed up late one night in 1969 to witness in awe the first steps of mankind on our moon. Little did I know then that I would later become associated with one of the primary persons responsible for allowing the world to watch this historic event as it happened, Efi Arazi.

By the time I became associated with Efi in the late 1990's, Efi had long left the space program and established himself as one of the great technology entrepreneurs of the twentieth century by founding and chairing two different billion dollar market cap companies, Electronics for Imaging and Scitex. Efi hired me as the senior finance officer for another start-up company in which he had become a major investor and chairman, Imedia Corporation. Imedia Corporation was soon sold for over one hundred million even though the company had less than two million of cumulative revenue. Subsequently I also had the pleasure and good fortune to work with Efi again on other early-stage projects.

Without a doubt Efi has been a great technology visionary, but I believe his true genius was greater than that. He did have several faults that could have left him a failure as an entrepreneur, but he had one strength that overcame all of these faults. He surrounded himself with the right people in the right roles at the right time for the organization.

Efi knew the keys to execution lay in the hands of the people he hired. Put the right people with the right skills and traits to work at the right time and the business plan will be improved and executed, and in the process a championship culture will be created. Anything less and the organization will stall. The task is complicated immensely by the simple facts of life that your financial resources are limited and staffing sucks up almost all of these resources. Therefore, your allocation of cash to build the management team and staff is an important constraining variable in the equation of placing the right people in the right roles at the right time.

Successful entrepreneurs have learned through trial and error that intelligently staffing the organization is as important as the technology the company develops and the market the company targets.

Based upon this context Section Two of this book digs into the horizontal staffing plan and other financial execution issues of the overall business plan. This chapter dissects the concept of intelligent staffing. The following chapter explores how options are used as an effective non-cash compensation vehicle to augment direct cash compensation. Chapter Ten continues with a discussion on how to set up an effective baseline internal financial control structure to coordinate the allocation of financial resources and to measure and control company wide financial performance. The final chapter discusses what I believe are the seven most common reasons entrepreneurs fail.

Traditional View of Staffing

Direct Staff

Board of Directors

Founder – Investor – Independent

Advisor Board

Industry – Functional

Consultants

Project – Interim – Part Time

Above the double line - primary focus is on differentiating activities.

Below the double line - primary focus is on non-differentiating activities.

Outsourced Functions

Legal – Tax Preparation – Bookkeeping – Human Resource Administration – Payroll – Information Systems – Technical Writing – Public Relations

Expanded View of Staffing

A Modern Definition of Staffing

Unseasoned entrepreneurs often think of staffing very narrowly. In the narrowest context, staff represents the people on the payroll. The seasoned entrepreneur realizes that staffing is a broader notion. Staff includes not only employees on the direct payroll, but also the Board of Directors, advisors, consultants and outsourced functions. This is not a legal definition, but rather a pragmatic definition that incorporates effective use of a diverse set of human resources to build the business.

Many entrepreneurs also incorrectly believe they should hire the executive team first, before solidly formulating their business and marketing plans. For example, let's say a company wants to hire a V.P of Marketing to help with the marketing portion of the business plan. Founders will often hire the wrong person because they are not yet sure where they want to take the company, nor are they sure which skills the candidate needs to help them get there.

> *Premature hiring sets the young company up for two very costly mistakes.*

Premature hiring sets up the young company for two very costly mistakes. First, if the company hires a full time V.P. of Marketing before understanding the marketing model, that marketing model will likely develop based upon the skills and accomplishments of the person the company has hired—not upon what the company needs. Second, if the company chooses a direction different from the skills and accomplishments of the marketing hire, then it has sunk the hiring costs and can look forward to the termination costs, replacement hire costs and the loss of precious time. Avoiding these mistakes requires doing homework and inclusion of board directors, advisors and consultants into your planning process.

The Board of Directors

The company's Board of Directors is legally responsible for governing the conduct of the company. The Board of Directors must exercise wisdom on decisions, including the decision to delegate other decisions to the operating management. Because of the "buck stops here" nature of these duties, both the company's founders and investors maintain the majority, if not all, of the available board seats. Therefore, carefully consider who will represent an investor on the company's Board of Directors and how much time they will commit to the company as important criteria for assessing the potential new lead investor.

> *Therefore, carefully consider who will represent an investor on the company's Board of Directors and how much time they will commit to the company as important criteria for assessing the potential new lead investor.*

If a board seat remains open the company can target an individual based on both the intangible and tangible benefit that person would bring to the table. One underused possibility is for the founders to nominate a non-founder to occupy one of their board seats. This decision is most useful when the founders are inexperienced and have built a relationship based upon trust with an experienced non-founder.

Board directors who are founders or investor representatives should receive no additional compensation. Board directors who are not from these groups typically receive compensation in the form of options. Options are discussed in detail in Chapter Nine – "Common Option Traps and Tricks." Your financial advisor (CFO or HR Consultant) should know what the appropriate compensation should be.

The Role of Advisors

As discussed above, opportunities to bring experienced board directors to the company are limited. In addition, no matter how involved your Board of Directors is, in all likelihood you will need additional help and support. Many companies have bridged this gap by creating an advisory board or boards. The relationship ranges from a formal board with standard meeting times and formats to informal one-on-one discussions.

Advisors can be targeted to provide industry knowledge or functional discipline assistance. Advisors with industry knowledge are useful for future market trend insights, product development support, as well as potential customer and investor introductions. Functional advisors are utilized to provide operational knowledge to guide organizational growth and to provide introductions. Common functional areas where advisors are retained include executive management, financial, legal, human resources, marketing, technical and operations.

Having an excellent team of advisors can also be useful in other ways. For example, advisors can assist in discussions outside of your core functional skills. Also, they can be a source of information and referrals. Industry and functional advisors filter information and resources, passing on those deemed appropriate for the company's review. In this regard they extend the reach of the organization into networks that the company would not otherwise be able to reach. For example, advisors may assist you in the development of candidate profiles for open positions, refer and screen candidates and refer you to other outside resources. Advisors can also be helpful when it comes to making decisions in tough situations—they have seen many mistakes made by others, and you can profit from their experiences.

Compensation for advisors consists primarily of Nonqualified Stock Options. Some companies use a portion of the common stock, subject to vesting and repurchase, in lieu of options. In general using common stock is a less favorable long-term compensation alternative and is only used if an option plan has not been established due to cash budget constraints. Functional advisors and industry advisors who perform services outside of a set number of hours, or who perform advisory services as an adjunct to a consulting practice, will likely require cash compensation on a time based or per project rate. Your attorney should have a standard advisor stock option grant agreement available for your use. Options are discussed in detail in Chapter Nine – "Common Option Traps and Tricks."

Effective Use of Consultants

Consultants work on a per project, part-time or interim position basis. Among the benefits of a seasoned consultant is practiced objectivity and experience in similar situations. During the business plan development phase consultants can often be used to help identify major decision points and the criteria necessary for the company to make informed decisions. Consultants can also be used appropriately to fill short-term skill requirements, e.g. new product development, interim executive management to raise a funding round, locating specific management team members, etc. The most prudent use of consultants is for short-term and part-time assignments.

One of the best ways to beef up the management team at a lower buy-in is to find an interim executive. This is especially useful when the executive you want to hire considers your company too risky to accept a full-time role. Seasoned consultants are adept at coming up to speed quickly, and therefore often need less time to achieve competence when compared to direct hires.

> *During the business plan development phase consultants can often be used to help identify major decision points and the criteria necessary for the company to make informed decisions.*

Not all consultants are created equal. Check references, ask tough questions and evaluate the chemistry. If you decide you want to move forward, thoroughly outline the engagement parameters, time commitment, deliverables, and payment milestones. Make sure a specific senior executive is responsible for monitoring the consultant's progress. Be sure you understand your internal time commitments as well. Consultants live by billing their time—make sure you note and agree to all of the project objectives and help the consultant get what he or she needs. Otherwise you will pay more and get less.

Most consultants have their own standard agreement and are reluctant to make modifications to it because they do not want additional legal fees on a per project basis. Nor do they relish managing several different agreement requirements (as opposed to project requirements). Agreements covering low dollar value engagements (under $20K to $50K depending upon your comfort zone) can probably be reviewed in house, while agreements covering high dollar value engagements should receive a legal checkup. Regardless of the size, all agreements should outline the deliverables, the payment triggers, ownership of intellectual property created, and the requirements of maintaining confidentiality. High dollar value agreements must also address performance and dispute resolution.

Outsourced Functions

Geoffrey A. Moore, in his book *Living on the Faultline*, discusses the role of internal functions versus outsourced functions. One basic point made in his discussion is that companies should retain and excel in functions and activities that provide or contribute to the current or future competitive advantage of the company. On the other hand, functions that do not meet this litmus test are candidates ripe for outsourcing.

The synopsis of this argument is "become an expert where it really matters, outsource to the external expert when it needs to be done efficiently and effectively." Outsourcing companies have embraced these "need to be done efficiently and effectively" functions as their claim to competitive advantage and are investing in them everyday to maintain their competitive advantage. Furthermore, in many cases these functions are simply not full-time tasks for an early-stage company. They will be performed either by a seasoned executive, thus taking away from his or her focus, or will be delegated to inexperienced lower level staff.

Functions that almost all early-stage companies should consider appropriate for outsourcing include legal, tax preparation, bookkeeping, human resource administration, payroll, information systems administration, technical writing, and public relations.

A specific note needs to be made in regard to attorneys, accounting firms and bankers. These firms often want to lock in the business of early-stage venture companies and will sometimes discount or defer fees to attract new client companies. It still can be feast or famine; in early 2000, as the Internet Bubble was peaking, I tried to get an audience with some of the well known providers in Silicon Valley and was told in one case that without at least $10M in venture funding already in the bank, they did not want to talk to the company I represented. In late 2001, having obviously changed their funding screen, this same firm is begging for business. Nonetheless, these three provider groups are usually much more in touch with the current dynamics and people in the venture funding business. Keep in mind that relationships with attorneys, accounting firms and bankers are usually long-term. Questions are asked when one of these relationships is changed; therefore considerable care should be given to understanding their capabilities and checking for positive chemistry prior to engagement.

Direct Staff

Invariably the bulk of your intermediate and long-term staffing efforts will be focused on the formal employees of the company, your direct staff. Obtaining the maximum value from each employee requires a commitment to hire and manage employees, treating the process as one of the company's top priorities.

Defining the Position – Define the Results Expected

Determining the qualifications of a position go hand in hand with determining the goals for and accomplishments required from the position. A common mistake is to create a position level and corresponding title that are over inflated for the actual duties to be performed (e.g. a VP title for director level duties, or a manager title for staff level duties).

First, this deflates the value of your organization in the eyes of other employees as well as your own Board of Directors, customers, investors and partners. If customers are in contact with someone who is not on par with the position title, your company's image suffers more than if you admit that you have a vacancy in the position. Second, this can create unnecessary future friction when an employee's title is deflated to make room for a new hire with the correct skills for the position level. Third, a modified reverse "Peter Principle" commonly occurs in early-stage growth companies.

> *Obtaining the maximum value from each employee requires a commitment to hire and manage employees, treating the process as one of the company's top priorities.*

The "Peter Principle," a concept advanced by Laurence Peters in his book *The Peter Principle*, refers to the tendency for employees to be promoted to their point of incompetence. Conversely, within early-stage growth companies the position's duties grow to the point where the employee is no longer competent in that position. For this reason successful companies should hire employees who are overqualified for the current position. Correctly defining the position requirements must incorporate an insightful understanding of the position's future requirements. Solicit input from experienced advisors or board directors to avoid this problem. Your challenge will be to attract quality candidates into a position that is below their current skill level.

> *However you decide to grow your company, you need to define its culture, management style, and communication style. The most successful companies hire people who can be successful in their workplace.*

In addition to the functional experience and skill sets, what domain requirements do you have for the position? Some companies actively target market spaces that are complementary to their own market space for a segment of the work force. This allows for some cross-pollination. In some cases, companies need to bring in people with expertise in areas where the company needs to blaze new ground. Many companies find the cross-pollination thought process important in building workforce diversity. Foreign companies who set up shop locally want to ensure that some key positions are filled by candidates familiar with local customs and resources. An additional benefit for the company is a culturally diverse workforce.

However you decide to grow your company, you need to define its culture, management style, and communication style. The most successful companies hire people who can be successful in their workplace. They create a list of characteristics common to the most successful people in the company and hire people with the same characteristics. Most employees who fail do so not because of the lack of skill or desire to be successful, but rather because their style clashes within the company that they are working for, and they cannot get things accomplished through other employees. For example, a budding software company with a loose management style and non-traditional work hours (10am-midnight) should probably avoid hiring someone from a manufacturing background who is accustomed to substantial structure and rules.

The probable cost of filling the position must also be addressed. Hard costs including recruiting fees, sign-on bonuses, relocation and salary are only part of the equation. Soft costs are also heavy and must be considered. These soft costs include the time needed to target, find and interview the chosen candidate, the new hire's time to competence, missed opportunities by not hiring quickly enough, and your current staff's time to build the new employee's competence. Early-stage companies often find the tradeoff of higher hard costs for a greater reduction of the soft costs both necessary and beneficial.

The Interview Process

Effective interviewing is a practiced art. Before an interview, perform or have your recruiter perform a phone screen based on criteria you have discussed. A few key questions can thresh out a lot of chaff. Second, learn to close interviews down if a negative outcome is apparent. Be aware that the position description often becomes modified based upon the education you receive from initial candidate interviews. Capitalize on this position testing to ensure you hire great candidates, but avoid radically changing your position description each time you find a candidate that you like. Recruitment professionals refer to this as the "candidate du jour" syndrome, i.e. you fall in love with each candidate you meet without respect to the company's overall organizational goals.

> *Interview questions are most effective when they are open ended in nature - that is they are designed to dig into the behavioral thought process of the candidate and cannot be answered by a "yes" or "no."*

Interview questions are most effective when they are open ended in nature—that is they are designed to dig into the behavioral thought process of the candidate and cannot be answered by a "yes" or "no." Behavioral interviewing is based upon the premise that past performance is the best indicator of future behavior. Instead of asking if candidate has experience in doing a process, ask them to describe their experience in accomplishing the process. Ask the candidate how he or she would approach a specific challenge. Look for competence in skills and accomplishments that are similar to the milestones that you need to meet. Also pay attention to attitudes and style to make sure you hire someone that will fit effectively with your current staff.

There are certain questions you may not legally ask in an interview process. In general, avoid asking personal questions and making judgments to avoid potential legal missteps. For example, do not ask, "Are you married?" Instead ask, "Do you foresee any complications in relocating quickly?" Do not ask, "Will your husband help you decide on whether or not you would accept this position?" Ask instead "What are the factors that will influence your decision on this position?"

When building your initial team, you can benefit by conducting interviews in a panel format. This allows the management team to observe each other, and uncover work styles, expected results, etc. Another benefit is that consensus for candidates becomes easier and subsequent non-panel interviews for other positions become more effective at selecting the best talent. As you build staff, including new members on panel interviews gives you the opportunity to mold their interviewing skills to select traits that embody your corporate culture—an important consideration as the company grows and your staff begins to lead the early stages of the hiring process. Nonetheless, senior management should have a final personal interview with candidates until it is no longer practical. This will vary from organization to organization; some companies have had the CEO involved for the first 500 employees. The average start-up company includes CEO involvement in hiring the first 100 employees and thereafter only for direct reports.

Do not forget to develop the proper paper protection trail for every candidate. The following items are the minimum requirements.

- A written position description.
- Unilateral Nondisclosure Agreement (NDA's) - to be signed by every candidate prior to discussion of proprietary information.
- A standard interview question area and response form to document each candidates interview performance.
- A standard release and authorization form for reference and credit checks.
- A standard reference check form to document responses to predetermined reference questions.
- The results of credit checks - all serious candidates should be investigated for credit and legal problems; red flags related to employee performance surface here. Note that legal requirements vary by state, to be safe have the prospective employee authorize the investigation in writing, and upon receipt of the investigative results, provide a copy to the prospective employee.
- A standard Employment At Will Offer Letter - explicitly outlining the initial functional duties and reporting structure of the position, the initial compensation, the right for either party to terminate the employment at will, and the companies policy on forced turnover (discussed subsequently in this chapter).
- A Proprietary Information and Invention Assignment Agreement.
- An employee option grant and disclosure document - used only if the company has adopted an option plan and after the Board of Directors has approved the employee's grant.
- An Under-Performance Notice form (discussed subsequently in this chapter).

Be sure to keep interview notes separate from the candidate's resume and employment file.

Packaging the Company to Prospective Employees

Actively consider how you are going to package and sell your company to prospective candidates. Just like your approach to a prospective customer, develop the winning pitch:

- Why are you the company they should bet their future on?
- Why is the management team capable of delivering?
- What are the company values?
- What is the company's business model and value proposition?

- Why is the target market appropriate?
- Who are the investors?

Do not underplay the risks involved, but do highlight the potential and show your confidence in the company's success and your faith in the management team, Board of Directors, investors, etc.

Outsourced Recruiting

Companies commonly find that, during their growth period, completion of all tasks necessary to pursue a staffing program is overwhelming. For direct staffing needs in a short time interval, a contract recruiter can work full time at your office to expedite the hiring program. This is the most cost effective outsourcing choice for hiring more than ten employees. A successful contract recruiter must be able to:

- Help the company determine staffing priorities.
- Help the company define each position and gauge the positions' current market compensation.
- Target and source appropriate candidates - especially identifying specific individuals in competitive companies when key industry specific knowledge is required.
- Screen candidates prior to an interview with management.
- Develop and oversee the interview process.
- Check references with the same behavioral approach used to interview candidates.
- Negotiate cost effective offers (within your guidelines) that still make candidates feel great about accepting the position.
- Follow up on employees after they have started to ensure they perform as expected.
- Collect and organize candidate documentation.
- Develop an overall efficient staffing process.

Each of the above steps requires the effective use of relationship sales skills. Finding a seasoned contract recruiter takes effort, but you will see a higher performance level compared to a less experienced contract recruiter.

Individual position searches can also be performed through contingent and retained search firms. Contingent firms are paid based upon their successful placement of a candidate. Consequently, they sometimes send in many candidates, some that may be unqualified and untested. It is seldom in their best interest to interview and screen candidates thoroughly because, for them, it is a numbers game. A significant amount of time must be dedicated to working with and managing contingent recruiters and therefore this type of recruiter is best used when someone inside the company has the time to undertake the relationship.

A retained recruiter is typically paid one third of his or her fee up front and should be reserved for exclusive searches of key executives. Because the relationship is exclusive and part of the fee is paid up front, a retained recruiter should be expected to perform at a higher level then a contingent recruiter. A retained recruiter should:

- Meet the entire executive team and board directors that are involved in the selection of candidates.
- Work with you to develop a position description that is based on expected results, candidate attributes and cultural fit.
- Interview pre-screened candidates in person and only forward the candidates that fit your open position.
- Perform complete background and reference checks on passing candidates.

Recruiters often specialize their practices in the functional areas and position levels, as well as the industries covered. When engaging a recruiter, find out who his or her clients are. It is important that you know where potential conflicts of interest lie, as the recruiter may not be able to get you the candidates you need if he or she has a lock out arrangement with one of your competitors. Also when working with a recruiter, make sure you understand what the fee is based on—first year salary, first year total compensation, or…? Your board directors, advisors and consultants will often know several recruiters that they have worked with successfully and are appropriate for a specific search.

Do not overlook your current employees as a valuable source for new candidates. Companies find that they frequently acquire better candidates from internal recommendations than they do from outside sources.

> *Companies find that they frequently acquire better candidates from internal recommendations than they do from outside sources.*

Offering to share some of the savings from the avoidance of an outside recruiting fee by giving employees a referral bonus can be a proposition profitable to company and employee alike. An effective method of structuring a referral bonus program is to pay half of the referral bonus on the first payroll following the referred employee's start, and the second half ninety days later.

Forced Turnover Programs

Many progressive established companies have adopted a formal forced turnover program. For example, even in its super growth period, Cisco attempted an annual layoff of the bottom performing five percent of their work force. Forced turnover programs aim both at motivating the majority of the employee base to strive for improvement and, simultaneously, at upgrading the employee base.

A formal forced turnover program is overkill for early-stage companies. However, the dual motivating and pruning principles should be part of every company's thought process. Pruning employees that are not performing to expectations will help motivate the high achievers by validating to the company's drive to be successful. In turn, by retaining high quality employees, you will attract more high quality employees.

Set the stage for a formal or informal turnover program as part of the offer letter. First, all employment should be "at will"—meaning that either the company or the employee can terminate the association without notice or cause. This is in compliance with California Employment Law (check your state for compatibility). Second, explicitly note that under-performing employees will be asked to leave the company. Unless you have covered an alternative method with your employment legal counsel, follow a standard three step termination process for an under performer:

- Notify the employee in writing of his or her need to improve using specific examples, list a time sensitive resolution plan (generally 30 to 60 days), and have the employee acknowledge the notice in writing. This is a formal Under-Performance Notice.
- Repeat the above process a second time if improvement does not occur as outlined in the first Under-Performance Notice (give only 30 days).
- Terminate the employee if the second notice has failed to produce the required results. You must pay the employee through the day of termination, including unused vacation or paid time off.

Conclusion

Intelligently staffing your company requires hard work and the consideration of available staffing possibilities, including your Board of Directors, advisors and consultants. You must spend the time to understand your business plan and the needs of the organization before incurring commitments for key position employees. Develop your company's hiring plan as a process to create a sustainable business, including the appropriate position definition, interviewing and attrition sub-processes.

Common Option Traps and Tricks

Options are a popular motivation tool for many employers. However, their limitations, as well as some of their capabilities, as incentives for employees are often misunderstood. Options are governed by two sets of complex and evolving rules, the federal tax code and generally accepted accounting principles. Most start-up companies adopt an Incentive Stock Option (ISO) plan as defined by the federal tax code. The majority of ISO plans also allow for granting of Nonqualified Stock Options (again as defined by the federal tax code) to non-employees. The Options Tax Treatment Summary Table on the following page summarizes the differences between ISO and Nonqualified Stock Options. Less popular, and therefore not addressed by this chapter, are Employee Stock Purchase Plans (ESPP's), which are commonly used by public companies. In any case, a company usually has a compensation attorney and a tax accountant develop the option plan and comment on it prior to adoption by the company's Board of Directors.

Basic Ingredients

Basic ingredients of ISO plans include the number of authorized shares and a standard vesting schedule. When an ISO plan is adopted, the company's board sets aside the number of authorized common shares available in the plan. The board determines the number of shares after considering what percentage of the company's equity should be devoted to the employee base as incentives. The number of shares and the percentage of equity devoted to the ISO plan are often interchangeably referred to as the size of the option pool.

Vesting refers to the rate at which an employee actually can own the stock free and clear, provided they pay the exercise price to the company. Probably the most common standard vesting schedule specifies a one-year cliff, or initial vesting after one year, of 25% of their grant, and 1/36th of the remaining shares every month thereafter. All vesting is calculated from the grant date. For example, an employee who started January 1st, 2001 and is granted options for 4,800 shares on January 15th, 2001 would vest 25% or 1,200 shares on January 15th, 2002 and an additional 100 shares on the 15th of each subsequent month through January 15th, 2005.

> *The exercise price set by the board represents their judgment of the current fair market value (FMV) of the common stock.*

All plans require an employee to exercise vested options within a set number of days after termination of employment, or within a set number of years from the original grant, if termination of employment has not occurred. If the employee does not exercise the option within these time frames, it is forfeited.

New employees are promised either a number of option shares or percent of the company. Take care to word the intention correctly if you promise a percentage in order to highlight the base used in calculating the percentage, i.e. total current diluted shares (all shares and potential shares including options, warrants and convertible loans) or total current undiluted shares (outstanding common and preferred stock only). Using the total undiluted shares as the base is an easier calculation to perform and recreate, however less shares are included in a specific promised option percentage grant.

The company's Board of Directors must also approve the individual grant, set the grant date, set the exercise price, and agree to the vesting schedule, as well as any additional special features of the specific option grant. The option grant date is usually the date of the board meeting or board action. The exercise price set by the board represents their judgment as to the current fair market value (FMV) of the common stock. Guidelines the board must use to determine the current FMV of the common stock are discussed later in this chapter under the topic of Cheap Stock.

> *Inexperienced management teams should "sanity-check" their option grant guidelines with independent sources; there's no sense in giving away options unnecessarily. It's also wise to have adequate options available to attract top management talent.*

Employees are not required to include the value of an ISO grant in their taxable income until the stock acquired by the exercise of that option is sold. However, all employees are deemed to have received Alternative Minimum Taxable Income (AMTI) when the option grant is exercised. AMTI is discussed in detail later in this chapter under the topic Alternative Minimum Taxable Income.

Options Tax Treatment Summary

Incentive Stock Options

Basic Requirements – Options Must be:
- For shares of employer corporation, it's parent or subsidiary, but not a sister corporation.
- Granted under a plan for a preset number of shares adopted by the corporation and approved by shareholders.
- Granted to employees (only) within ten years of the plan's adoption or approval, whichever occurs first.
- Exercisable within ten years of grant date.
- At a price equal to or exceeding the fair market value of the stock at the time of grant.
- Not be transferable except upon death of the employee (generally up to the employee and spouse to resolve a workaround in divorce cases).
- Exercised within three months of employment termination.
- The employee cannot own, at the time of grant, shares representing more than ten percent of the voting control in the employer corporation, it's parent or any subsidiary.
- Subject to $100K annual first time per calendar year exercise limit, excess reclassified to Nonqualified Stock Option.

Tax Treatment for the Individual
- Not treated as taxable income when granted.
- Not treated as taxable income when exercised.
- Included in Alternative Minimum Taxable Income (AMTI) when exercised, becomes a negative AMTI adjustment when the stock is sold.
- Gain or loss from the sale of shares acquired by option exercise is taxable as ordinary income if capital gains treatment criteria are not met.
- Gain or loss from the sale of shares acquired by option exercise is taxable as capital gains income if sold after one year of exercise and two years after the option grant.
- Loss from the sale of shares acquired by option exercise is not allowed if a wash sale occurs (i.e. within thirty days before or after the sale a purchase of the stock or an option of substantially the same form is acquired).

Tax Treatment for the Corporation
- No tax deduction is allowed upon the grant or exercise of the option.
- Required to track and report early dispositions (sales of shares acquired by option exercise that do not meet holding period for capital gains treatment as defined above).

Nonqualified Stock Options

Basic Requirements
- Option does not qualify as an Incentive Stock Option (as defined at left).

Tax Treatment for the Individual
- Generally not treated as taxable income upon grant (Nonqualified Stock Options must have a readily ascertainable fair market value at the time of grant to be treated as taxable income at the time of grant, private companies rarely meet this requirement).
- Treated as taxable income at the time of exercise (exercise price less option price).
- Subsequent sales of shares acquired are subject to capital gains tax treatment.

Tax Treatment for the Corporation
- A deduction is allowed equal to and coincident with the taxable income recognized by the individual.

Nonqualified Stock Options typically are granted to consultants or advisors (any person or organization who is not on the company's direct payroll) as part of their compensation for services previously rendered. Vesting has thus occurred, but a requirement to exercise the option within a set period from the grant date is still imposed. Grant dates and exercise prices are determined in the same manner as with ISO's. The FMV of Nonqualified Stock Options at the grant date is not usually considered income to the recipient. The receipt does recognize ordinary income at the time of option exercise equal to the difference between the current FMV and the exercise price.

In addition to the tax treatment distinctions between ISO and Nonqualified Stock Options, there are also accounting distinctions between the two. ISO options may be accounted for using an "intrinsic" value model (measurement process), which most companies use, or a "fair" value model (measurement process). Nonqualified Stock Options must always be accounted for using the "fair" value model. Rather than dissecting the complete descriptions of each model, I will directly discuss the accounting impacts on a topic-by-topic basis.

Common Traps

Option Grant Guidelines

A fairly common trap that inexperienced management teams fall into is the failure to set guidelines that establish parity between a individual's position level and importance to the company, and to factor those guidelines into the projected staffing needs of the company and the total size of the option pool. Management should develop option grant guidelines (perhaps in a matrix format) to avoid this trap. An example of an options planning matrix is shown on the following page. Your Board of Directors will often increase the number of authorized shares in the option pool one year after a funding round, in order to restore the total option pool percentage back to the targeted level. Therefore, the time frame that an option grant guideline must cover becomes manageable. Inexperienced management teams should "sanity check" their option grant guidelines with independent sources; there's no sense in giving away options unnecessarily. It's also wise to have adequate options available to attract top management talent.

Quicksilver Sample, Inc.
Options Grant Guidelines
Effective January 1st, 2001

Midrange of guideline is used for option pool planning.

Guideline percentage ranges will be adjusted downward as Quicksilver Sample, Inc. progresses.

Additional option grants under the informal evergreen program are at 1/4 (25%) of the range indicated.

C, VP and Board of Director grants are individually determined.

Current outstanding equivalent common shares   10,000,000

		Director			Manager			Advisor		
		High	Mid	Low	High	Mid	Low	High	Mid	Low
Professional Management	% of current outstanding equivalent common shares	1.25%	1.00%	0.75%	0.80%	0.65%	0.50%	0.50%	0.38%	0.25%
	Number of shares	125,000	100,000	75,000	80,000	65,000	50,000	50,000	38,000	25,000
		Senior			Staff			Junior		
		High	Mid	Low	High	Mid	Low	High	Mid	Low
Engineering	% of current outstanding equivalent common shares	0.80%	0.65%	0.50%	0.60%	0.50%	0.40%	0.40%	0.30%	0.20%
	Number of shares	80,000	65,000	50,000	60,000	50,000	40,000	40,000	30,000	20,000
		Senior			Staff			Junior/Clerical		
		High	Mid	Low	High	Mid	Low	High	Mid	Low
Other Staff	% of current outstanding equivalent common shares	0.60%	0.50%	0.40%	0.40%	0.30%	0.20%	0.15%	0.10%	0.05%
	Number of shares	60,000	50,000	40,000	40,000	30,000	20,000	15,000	10,000	5,000

119

Cheap Stock

> *Exercise prices for options are almost always set at a discount to the last preferred round stock price, due to the inherent liquidation preference and other protections built into the preferred stock.*

Another common trap, this time created by generally accepted accounting principles, which snares successful companies who have survived the formative years and become IPO candidates, is called "cheap stock." Cheap stock refers to options granted to an employee at an exercise price that is less than the common shares' fair value at the time of the grant. Having your option grants classified as cheap stock creates the requirement to show non-cash compensation expenses on your profit and loss statement over time equal to the excess of the fair value of the common stock over the option's exercise price if the "intrinsic value" rather than the "fair value" model is used for accounting purposes. The cheap stock non-cash compensation expense is spread out over the entire vesting period of the options.

There is no guaranteed method for avoiding this trap. However, you can take steps to minimize any potential impact. First, regularly discuss the issue with your audit firm to gauge the latest experiences of companies undergoing a review by the Securities and Exchange Commission (SEC) during their pre-IPO registration period. The SEC invariably requests a company in the IPO process to substantiate the fair values assigned to common stock issuances and option grants made during the twelve months preceding the date of the most recent financial statements included in the registration statement. In the evaluation of the fair value of the stock or grant, the company should consider the proximity of the issuance to the proposed public offering, intervening events, transfer restrictions and exercise dates, and profitability and financial condition of the company. The SEC looks to objective evidence as the best support for the determination of fair value, such as transactions with third parties involving issuances of stock for cash and appraisals by reputable independent valuation experts. Second, your Board of Directors should closely examine the progress of the company and the factors that currently differentiate the risk reward ratio of the company's common stock versus the preferred stock.

Many early-stage companies, incorrectly, simply peg the current common stock price as a factor of the most recent preferred round stock price, and as the time before an IPO appears short, the expected IPO share price. The common stock price may start out close to a 1 to 10 ratio of your seed round preferred stock price and gradually move towards a 1 to 1 ratio during each successive stock round. For example, the price ratio may be set at 1:6 at the Series B Preferred Stock round, at a 1:4 ratio at the Series C Preferred Stock round, and so on. Exercise prices for options are almost always set at a discount to the last preferred round stock price, due to the inherent liquidation preference and other protections built into the preferred stock.

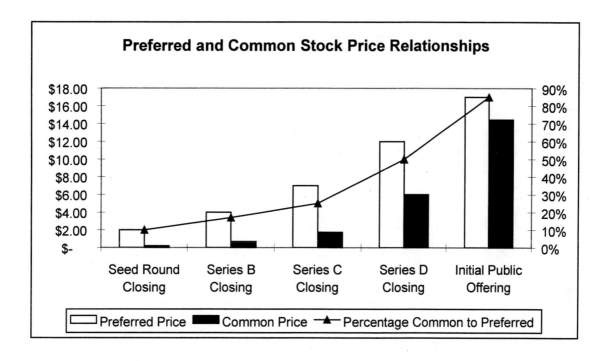

Although the common stock price is almost always set at a discount to the most recent preferred stock price, and the pattern often appears to look as discussed above, the Board of Directors must be careful to document the progress assessment, risk and reward factors that justify each pricing decision. The SEC will reject valuations that rely on undocumented or unsubstantiated "rules of thumb;" for example, the use of a fixed percent of the most recent third party preferred stock share price to value common stock, or the use of general rules of thumb for lack of marketability and/or minority interest discount in fair market value.

Avoiding Variable Options

Most companies want to keep options granted to employees under their ISO plan to be considered "fixed" as opposed to "variable." Fixed and variable options are another distinction stemming from generally accepted accounting principles that apply to options granted to employees (board directors are considered employees under this distinction while advisors and consultants are not considered employees). A fixed option implies that all option terms regarding the price and number of shares are set up-front. Any modification in price reclassifies the option into a variable option. This distinction is important because the date for measuring compensation for a fixed option is the date of grant whereas the measurement date for a variable option will be later, typically when a performance milestone is achieved or a contingent event occurs. Hence, it is easier with a fixed option to avoid compensation cost for accounting purposes because the exercise price can be set to equal the fair value of the underlying stock at the date of grant. This ability is lacking with a variable option because at the date of grant it is impossible to predict what fair value will be on the future measurement date. The compensation charge associated with a variable option must be recalculated at every external reporting period if it is judged probable that the future event that fixes the number of shares and the exercise price will occur.

Option Accounting (Financial Reporting) Treatment For Options Granted to Employees

Fixed Option Plan Defined
Basic Requirements

- In a fixed option plan both the number of shares an individual is entitled to receive and the option price are fixed (i.e. known).

Variable Option Plan Defined
Basic Requirements

- In a variable option plan the number of shares to be received or the exercise price are not known at the date of grant, i.e. they are dependent upon the occurrence of a future event.

Compensation Expense Treatment

- A fixed option plan does not require the recording of compensation expense for accounting purposes if the option price is equal to the current fair market value of the stock at the time of grant.

Compensation Expense Treatment

- The measurement of compensation cost for a variable option will vary with changes in fair value of the underlying stock (and sometimes other factors) until the date the number of shares to be granted and the exercise price are both known.

Re-pricing an option exercise price used to be a common practice; it was done when a company experienced a valuation change that caused the FMV of the common stock to fall below an option's exercise price. The exercise price of the option was reset to the current FMV as a trade-off for restarting the vesting period. However, since the re-pricing now kicks the option into the variable category, re-pricing is much less attractive as a strategy.

A loan to an employee, for the purpose of exercising their stock options, can also cause the option to be classified as a variable option—if, for example, the interest rate of the loan is below a current market rate at the time of exercise. Proper use of option loans is discussed later in this chapter under "Option Loan."

Accounting Issues Related to Options for Non Employees

Most companies account for stock-based compensation awards using the "intrinsic" value model rather than a fair value model. Fixed and variable options exist in the context of the "intrinsic" value model. Options granted to advisors and consultants (and other dilutive securities such as warrants for investors) must always be valued for accounting purposes using a fair value measurement process. This process usually involves a Black-Scholes option-pricing model to determine the options value, and the resulting value is amortized over the options vesting period. Software to perform the Black-Scholes calculation can be readily found on the Internet.

Incentive Stock Option Limitation

If during any one calendar year an employee becomes eligible to exercise for the first time options valued at more than $100K, based on the FMV at the date of grant, the excess over $100K is reclassified to a Nonqualified Stock Option. For example, an employee who has been granted 80,000 options at $5 a share under a four year vesting schedule comprised of a one-year cliff followed by $1/48^{th}$ of the original amount per month thereafter will be subject to reclassification in the year the cliff terminates (unless the termination occurs in December). Over $100K (calculated by 80,000 options times twenty-five percent times $5) will become exercisable during one calendar year.

Employees with acceleration clauses or pre-purchase rights (both discussed later in this chapter) can also be unexpectedly caught in this trap.

Alternative Minimum Taxable Income (AMTI)

For employees the biggest options related trap is the generation of AMTI upon the exercise of an option. AMTI is an alternative method for determining the income tax owed to the federal, and in some cases, the state government. When the AMTI legislation was first incorporated into the tax code very few individuals were subject to the alternative tax calculation. However as with other tax complications the time bomb has caught up with many more individuals. AMTI considers certain non-cash events as income and reduces some common itemized deductions.

With ISO exercises AMTI is calculated as the difference between the extended FMV on the date of exercise and the extended exercise price of the options. The only way to avoid AMTI is to sell the stock (without creating a wash sale) prior to the end of the employees tax year (the tax year is usually the same as the calendar year) in which the option was exercised.

In severe cases during 2000 where the stock market crumbled, some public company key executives actually had to quit their position with a company in order to sell stock acquired earlier in the year, which at year-end was trading below their exercise price. Quitting was necessary in these cases, because the block-out periods for insiders of publicly held companies prevented them from selling the acquired stock while they were still an employee of the company.

Although AMTI cannot be avoided, it can be reduced to zero with proper planning as discussed later in this chapter under Pre-Purchase Rights.

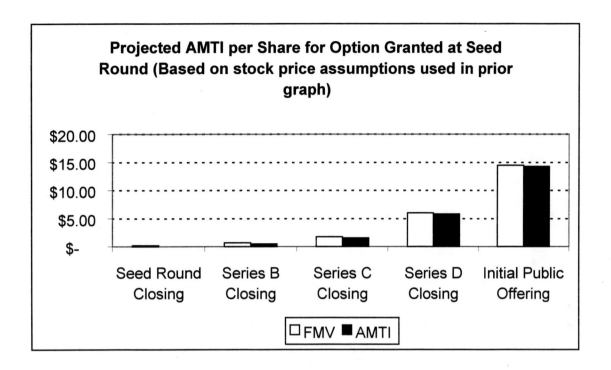

Projected AMTI per Share for Option Granted at Seed Round (Based on stock price assumptions used in prior graph)

Reverse-Splits

Some companies unintentionally end up with too many shares outstanding at the point they are ready to file for an IPO. Although too many shares outstanding may first sound like an oxymoron, the experience can cause serious morale problems with employees. As an underwriter reviews a company that is considering an IPO, one consideration is the projected offering price per share, calculated by dividing the expected market valuation that the company will receive by the number of shares outstanding after the offering. Underwriters generally like to price shares sold in an IPO at double-digits; therefore, if their calculation results in a share price under $10, they will request the company to perform a reverse-split to reduce the number of shares. Thus, 10 shares can be reverse-split into 1 share.

The reverse-split does not change the company's total value, and each shareholder still owns the same percentage before and after the split. However, when an employee sees an option grant for 10,000 shares reverse-split into an option grant for 1,000 shares, they automatically feel that the value of their options is now 10% of what they had — it's a purely psychological phenomenon, but the effect is devastating to morale. Often these employees have already calculated the value of their pre-split shares at the $10 per share price.

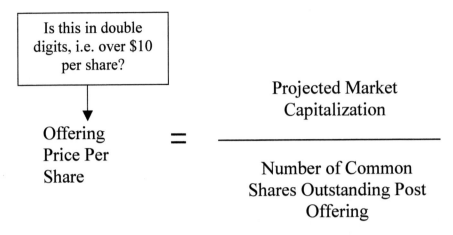

Offering Price Per Share Projection

Foreign-Based Employees

Employees based in foreign countries are often subject to international corporate and tax laws that create radically different effects. Option plans that will include foreign-based employees should be reviewed for compliance and effectiveness within the employee's home country.

Useful Tricks

Evergreen Programs

An Evergreen Program matches a new option grant, at the current FMV, to the vesting schedule of an existing option grant. Thus an employee maintains the same total number of unvested option shares as an incentive. A formal Evergreen Program is overkill for most start-up companies. However, use of an informal program that provides new option grants for all employees (based on each employee's value to the organization) at a common annual date can easily be adopted. The informal Evergreen Program allows valuable employees to be rewarded in a non-cash format. Remember to include the informal Evergreen Program into the option planning guidelines established for the total option pool.

Acceleration

A properly created option plan can allow the acceleration of option vesting for specific individuals — or all employees based on a preset milestone event. The most common milestone event that is used to trigger an acceleration event is a merger of the company, where the shareholders before the merger retain less than 50% of the surviving company's ownership. The purpose of an acceleration event is to motivate and reward employees during the merger transition.

Accelerations can be implemented on an individual basis for select employees by writing the acceleration into their contract or employment offer. Companies who believe a sale is likely may choose to incorporate the acceleration into each option grant. Accelerations may be pegged to a percentage of the unvested option shares (e.g. ½ of the unvested options) or pegged to length of employment with the company (e.g. an additional ¼ of the initial option grant per year of service).

Note that a portion of an Incentive Stock Option can be reclassified to a Non-qualified Stock Option if the acceleration creates a situation where over $100K worth of options, measured by the fair market value on the grant date, is exercisable for the first time in any one calendar year due to the acceleration. This issue was discussed early in this chapter under Incentive Stock Option Limitation.

If vesting is accelerated based on the occurrence of a specific event or condition in accordance with the original terms of the option grant, no new measurement of compensation cost is required for accounting purposes.

> *The most common milestone event used to trigger an acceleration event is a merger of the company, where the shareholders before the merger retain less than 50% of the surviving company's ownership.*

Pre-Purchase (Early Exercise) Rights

Key employees may request the right to pre-purchase the option grant, subject to repurchase of unvested shares if termination of employment occurs. If the plan allows for pre-purchase rights then all employees with options can take advantage of these rights. The pre-purchase is especially advantageous to the key employee for two reasons.

First, if the proper "83B" election notices are completed and delivered to the IRS and the company, the employee can specify that the valuation date of the FMV for the stock acquired by the option exercise is to be set at the pre-purchase date. If the election forms are not properly filed, the valuation date will be the date the employee owns the acquired stock free and clear. Presuming the pre-purchase is performed within a short period from the option grant, the AMTI calculation (discussed previously in this chapter) results in a zero or minimal AMTI amount.

Secondly, the capital gains period for the stock ownership begins on the pre-purchase date (an employee must hold the stock for one year from exercise date and two years from grant date in order to receive capital gains treatment on a sale).

One potential drawback to the company is that the repurchase of unvested shares becomes an additional liability of the company to the employee if the company needs to reduce staff in tight times.

Note that a portion of an Incentive Stock Option can be reclassified to a Nonqualified Stock Option if the pre-purchase right creates a situation where over $100K worth of options, measured by the fair market value on the grant date, is exercisable for the first time in any one calendar year due to the pre-purchase rights. This issue was discussed early in this chapter under Incentive Stock Option Limitation.

Option Loan

Key employees may also request a loan to allow them to exercise options with a pre-purchase right. Provided the loan is full recourse to all assets of the employee and the interest rate meets or exceeds a fair market rate this arrangement generally does not cause compensation expense for accounting purposes. Market interest rates are not explicitly defined in the accounting rules, however if the rate is equal to the rate available on a margin stock brokerage account you are probably safe.

The interest rate of the loan must also fall within IRS guidelines to avoid potential tax implications. In general if you meet the criteria for a market interest rate per the accounting rules then the interest rate should be acceptable for the IRS. Alternatively, the interest amounts can be forgiven when due, provided the employee's W-2 reflects the amount of forgiven interest as additional compensation.

Common Traps and Tricks Summary Table

Name	Affects Who	Positive or Negative	Source of Trap or Trick	Offset Method By or For
Common Traps				
Options Grant Guidelines	Company (ability to recruit)	N	Poor Planning	Capital & Staff Planning
Cheap Stock	Company	N	Accounting Rules	Corporate Governance and Planning
Variable Options	Company	N	Accounting Rules	Corporate Governance and Planning
Below Market Options	Company	N	Accounting Rules	Corporate Governance and Planning
Incentive Stock Option Limitation	Individual	N	Federal Tax ode	Limiting Acceleration and Pre-Purchase Rights
Alternative Minimum Income Tax (AMTI)	Individual	N	Federal Tax Code	Pre-Purchase Rights, Option Loans
Reverse Splits	Individual	N	Poor Planning	Capital Planning
Foreign Based Employees	Potentially Both	N	Foreign Corporate and Tax Laws	International Legal and Tax Planning
Common Tricks				
Evergreen Program	Both	P	N/A	Capital and Staff Planning
Acceleration	Individual	P	Accounting Rules	N/A, Creates possible Incentive Stock Option Limitation
Pre-Purchase Rights	Individual	P	Federal Tax Code	AMTI, Creates possible Incentive Stock Option Limitation
Option Loan	Individual	P	Federal Tax Code	AMTI

Conclusion

Option plans can powerfully motivate employees and allow them to participate in a young company's financial growth. The company must be aware of and avoid potential traps that create negative accounting, personal income tax and other impediments to this important employee motivation. Several methods exist to provide key employees with extra benefits to increase the value of their option grants. Implementation and active stewardship of an ISO plan require the support of expert professionals. A summary of the traps and tricks discussed within this chapter was presented on the previous page.

Companies interested in maximizing employee value through their option program often host a voluntary informational workshop during non-work hours. This type of workshop usually involves presentation and discussion lead by a non-employee expert on options issues. A disclaimer that the company is not an advisor to the employee in these matters should be included in the presentation.

For those who really want to dig into the rules and regulations behind these concepts the sources of the generally accepted accounting principles are Accounting Principals Board (APB) Option No. 25, Financial Accounting Standards Board Statement of Financial Accounting Standards (FAS) No. 123, Financial Accounting Standards Board Interpretation (FIN) No. 44 and Emerging Issues Task Force (EITF) Issue No. 96-18 and Issue No. 00-23. Governing sections of the Federal Tax Code are Sections 83 and 421 through 424.

Creating a Baseline Internal Financial Control Structure

At some point each successful entrepreneur must begin to rely on effective process control structures for assurance that the company will continue to run smoothly forward. Reliance is possible only when you know the true results of the operations on a timely basis, and you have put in place a workable financial control structure to *minimize* unfavorable and unauthorized business events along with intentional and unintentional errors. The word minimize is used because, even in the best of circumstances, total elimination is neither possible nor affordable.

Whether your basic financial staffing plan centers on in-house employees, outsourced financial and accounting functions, or a combination of both, setting the appropriate expectations from the function must be done to achieve real results. In the paragraphs following this introduction I show the basic building blocks your early-stage company can use to develop the foundation for proper internal financial control.

Authorization Matrix

As a first step, the company should clearly document and communicate to all employees the authority delegated to themselves and other members of the organizational team. A clear, simple method to accomplish this task is by using an Authorization Matrix. Since all early stage companies must remain responsive to changing business dynamics the Authorization Matrix should be updated periodically as circumstances within the company dictate. An ideal Authorization Matrix is comprehensive in coverage and still concise enough to fit on one page (and still be readable). Employees engaged in accounting, purchasing and similar backend functions must also be explicitly instructed that as a function of their role they are responsible to bring forward abuses of authority for senior management action. Concurrently, management must support this ethical accountability with proper corrective action on observed abuses.

131

> *Clearly document and communicate to all employees the authority delegated to them and other members of the organizational team.*

Develop an Authorization Matrix by listing management levels across the top and the commitment types on the left. For example, the across the top start with the following columns: All Employees, Managers, Directors, Vice Presidents, and CEO. Label the rows with the types of commitments you need to control: Purchase Orders, New Hires, etc. Then complete the matrix boxes with the authority you wish to delegate and list the effective date of the Authorization Matrix on the document.

Make sure you put the control at the front end of the transaction (the commitment) and not on the back end (the payment or collection).

Chart of Accounts

The Chart of Accounts is another basic building block of an effective internal financial control structure. All too often I have reviewed financial statements that exhibit simple structural errors that would have been easily prevented by a simple Chart of Accounts. Common simple structural errors include:

- Inconsistent use of accounts.
- Large numbers of unrelated transactions lumped in the same account.
- Significant expense items improperly segregated to foster analysis.
- Accounts used only for one or two nonmaterial transactions.
- No parity with the categorizations used in financial plans.

Adopting a simple Chart of Accounts that not only lists the authorized accounts but also includes a basic description of the account's proper use will prevent these problems. Transaction error rates will decrease definitely and management will understand a specific account's significance and use – and is far better prepared to obtain a meaningful performance overview.

With a little added work the account descriptions can be embellished to delineate calculation methods, company policies (e.g. travel guidelines, excess cash investment policy, cross department charges, fixed asset purchasing), and procedural methods. The basic key is to create and use the Chart of Accounts as a standard communication vehicle.

Quicksilver Sample, Inc.
Authorization Matrix

Date:	20-Aug-01
Revision:	1.1
Scope:	Company Wide
Owner:	CFO

The following table applies to the entire commitment, irrespective of individual invoicing.

Other specific policies may also apply, e.g. as for purchasing personal computers.

		Staff	Department Manager or Director	Vice President	CEO or COO	Requires Joint Sign Off by CFO	Requires Joint Sign Off by Director of Human Resources
Department Commitments	Department Purchases - Within current quarters budget 1)	< $500	< $1,000	< $2,000	>= $2,000		
	Department Purchases - Not within current quarters budget		< $1,000	< $2,000	>= $2,000	Yes	
	Supplier Terms Modifications 2)		All			Yes	
	Travel Authorization - total expected cost, travel per company policy 3)		< $1,000	< $2,000	>= $2,000	Any proposed exception to travel policy	
	Fixed Assets			< $2,000	>= $2,000	Yes	
Customers	Customer Credit Limits/Currency				All	Yes	
	Credit & Shipping Terms Modifications 4)					All	
	Pricing Tables				All		
	Customer Concessions				All	Yes	
Personnel	Internal Sales Commissions - Program				All	Yes	Yes
	Internal Sales Commissions - Calculations & Payout				All	Yes	
	New Hires/Terminations/Salary Adjustments				All		Yes
Inventory	Sales Forecast - For MRP Generation				All	Yes	
	Inventory - MRP Generated based upon approved Sales Forecast	< $10,000	>= $10,000 Director of Operations only				
	Inventory - non MRP Generated		< $2,000 Director of Operations only		>= $2,000	>= $2,000	
Contracts	Contracts - Under One Year and total value is …		< $1,000	< $2,000	>= $2,000	>= $2,000	
	Contracts - Over One Year				All	Yes	

1) Purchase orders are not required by Quicksilver Sample, Inc. for purchases under $500.

2) Standard Supplier Terms are net 30 from later of receipt or invoice.

3) All travel authorization and expense reports are to be approved by the next level manager regardless of total cost.

4) Standard Credit Terms are established by customer, all sales are FOB Mountain View and invoiced in US Dollars.

Note: only examples of some common accounts are included in this illustration.

Quicksilver Sample, Inc
Consolidated Chart of Accounts

Date:	April 25th, 2001
Revision:	1.4
Scope:	Company Wide
Owner:	Ed Snate
	CFO

Purpose

The Consolidated Chart of Accounts serves as the guide governing consistent company wide recording of accounting activity by individual account. The Consolidated Chart of Accounts also outlines accepted Company Policy relative to accounting methods and business processes.

New Accounts

Suggestions for new accounts should be forwarded the CFO. The CFO will decide if a new account is required, or whether an existing account is appropriate.

Balance Sheet Accounts

1000   *Petty Cash*
Use - Accounting
Classification – Cash

> Petty Cash accounts are maintained on an impress basis and therefore, are pre-set at authorized balances. The CFO must approve changes in authorized amounts. Normally, this account will not carry a balance over the equivalent of U.S. $1,000.

1010   *Main Checking Account*
Use – Accounting
Classification – Cash

> This account is used for the main checking activity of Quicksilver Sample, Inc. All funds are demand deposits available for withdrawal by check or other means without notice. Balances in this account are normally non-interest bearing.

> Company policy requires two authorized signatures for disbursements over twenty thousand USD. Transfers between accounts require initiation and confirmation by separate authorized employees.

1400   *Capitalized Equipment*
1460   *Leasehold Improvements*
Use - Everyone
Extract – General Distribution
Classification –Fixed Assets

> These accounts are used to record all capitalized fixed assets acquired by Quicksilver Sample Inc. An item classified in this account must have:
> a)   an initial cost of greater than U.S. $1,000, and
> b)   have a projected useful life in excess of one year,
> All capitalized assets are depreciated straight line on the lesser of its usable life or five years (three years for computer equipment, automobiles or trucks, trade booths and production equipment). All

leasehold improvements are amortized over the shorter of the underlying lease term or their useful life (generally not longer than five years). All transactions charged to a capitalized asset account must reference the department responsible for custody of the asset.

1490   *Accumulated Depreciation and Reserve*
Use - Accounting
Classification - Fixed Assets (contra)

> Used to accumulate the depreciation of all general fixed assets in the corresponding 14XX accounts, except *Leasehold Improvements* (account 1460). Quicksilver Sample Inc.'s depreciable life criteria are discussed above. The account is also used to accumulate reserves for assets in the corresponding 14XX accounts where the expected life of the equipment no longer matches the original assumption and therefore suggests an inherent financial exposure. Changes to the reserve in this account require the CFO's approval.

2225   *Deferred Revenue*
Use - Accounting
Classification - Other Current Liabilities

> Used to record revenue that cannot be recognized before the future performance of contractual obligations, except normal obligations to perform under an initial product warranty.

Profit and Loss Accounts

4000   *Licensing Revenue*
Use - Sales
Extract – General Distribution
Classification – Revenue

> Gross revenue attributed to the current period from the license of Quicksilver Sample, Inc.'s technology to an unrelated party.

4100   *Product Revenue*
Use - Sales
Extract – General Distribution
Classification – Revenue

> Gross revenue attributed to the current period from the sale of products to an unrelated party.

4200   *Service Revenue*
Use - Sales
Extract – General Distribution
Classification – Revenue

> Gross revenue attributed to the current period from the installation, training and service to an unrelated party.

4210   *Extended Warranty & Customer Support Revenue*
Use - Sales
Extract – General Distribution
Classification – Revenue

> Gross revenue received from extended warranty and customer support programs. Revenue is recognized on a prorated basis through the life of the obligation (reference account 2220 *Accrued Warranty & Customer Support*).

Departmental Expense Accounts

Normally departmental expense accounts are reflected as Cost of Goods Sold (Operations Department) or Operating Expenses (all departments except Operations) on the Profit and Loss Statement. Until Quicksilver Sample, Inc.'s product is sold to customers; the Operations department is included within Operating Expenses.

6120 *Employee Compensation*
Use - Accounting
Extract – General Distribution
Classification - Personnel & Related Departmental Expense
> Payments to employees of Quicksilver Sample, Inc. for normal salary, overtime premium, holiday pay, retroactive salary adjustments, and liability adjustments corresponding to paid time off (PTO) liability. All amounts are recorded gross of employee paid taxes and other deductions withheld by the employer.

6310 *Meals*
Use - Everyone
Extract – General Distribution
Classification – Travel Departmental Expense
> Expenses related to providing meals while an employee is engaged in business activities whether while traveling or while working at the company office. Meals with customers or vendors are classified as Entertainment and recorded in account 6320.

6320 *Entertainment*
Use - Everyone
Extract – General Distribution
Classification – Travel Departmental Expense
> Expenses related to entertainment (including business meals) while an employee is engaged in business activities with customers or vendors.

6330 *Airfare*
Use - Everyone
Extract – General Distribution
Classification – Travel Departmental Expense
> The direct cost of airfares and associated landing/departure taxes included directly in the cost of the airline ticket for employees traveling on company business.

6340 *Lodging*
Use - Everyone
Extract – General Distribution
Classification – Travel Departmental Expense
> Expenses related for lodging at a hotel or related facilities incurred by an employee while traveling on company business. Incidental expenses (e.g. laundry) incurred while traveling should also be recorded in this account.

6555 *Safety Certification, Licenses & Permits*
Use – Engineering and Administration
Extract – General Distribution
Classification – Product Development Departmental Expense
> Expenses for obtaining laboratory safety certification on Quicksilver Sample, Inc.'s products and technology or manufacturing licenses and permits.

Financial Statements

Financial Statements serve as the feedback loop to inform the management of the company's financial performance. In order for the feedback loop to provide the greatest value, the financial statements must be both timely and distributed to those responsible for the results.

> *There is just no acceptable excuse for a company not to have full knowledge of the monthly results within in a few working days from the period end.*

The tired old practice of generating financial statements several weeks after a period end is passé. Current, easy to use and affordable, entry level software such as QuickBooks Pro or Peachtree eliminates the mundane, time consuming ticking and tying of the pre-computer era. Reoccurring entries (entries that occur for the same amount or a precalculated amount each month) and reversing entries (accrual entries that are reversed the following month when actual data is available or processed) can be performed prior to months end. Issues requiring expertise beyond the preparer's knowledge can be discussed with the appropriate professional advisor and resolved prior to month end as well. There is just no acceptable excuse for a company not to have full knowledge of the monthly results within a few working days from the period end, especially if complex manufacturing or similar activities are not part of your company's normal business. When this does not occur, management has not demanded and emphasized that untimely reporting is unacceptable.

As outlined above, preparing punctual and accurate financial statements is not enough. The financial statements must be circulated and reviewed with the management team – even if this means that the preparer seeks out the management team. This review must include a discussion of the actual results versus the financial plan and an agreement to modify either financial behavior or the financial plan to eliminate a perpetuation of undesired variances. Questions such as "What was our true burn rate?" or "What is in this account?" should not be unanswered at the end of the management review process.

Account Reconciliation's

Up to date knowledge and agreement of the underlying items within each balance sheet account should not be a monumental task. On the contrary, consistent review combined with fostering the underlying accuracy of the transactions greatly helps the reconciliation task. Reconciliation of the bank accounts, subledger agreement to payables and receivables accounts, and spreadsheet recaps of less active accounts should be easy to maintain. In some cases, for example fixed assets, keeping an account binder copy of the transactional paperwork is a good investment for efficient future reference.

In many start-up companies the employee responsible for payments is also responsible for reconciliation of key related accounts, i.e. bank accounts and payables, payroll processing and payroll recording. Wherever this situation exists the opportunity for fraud is greater. Even if a key manager is signing vendor checks, the opportunity for a forged check to slip though unnoticed still exists. Larger companies have traditionally created a separation of duties in these areas by incorporating the use of multiple individuals in different functional capacities to serve as the check and balance. Smaller companies often do not have this luxury. This reinforces the need for management review and understanding of the financial statements and key account reconciliation's to compensate as a substitute check and balance.

Payables Planning

Warning signs of poor payables planning include rush checks, over or underpaid bills, double payments, lost discounts, early payments and vendor calls routed to management. If these events are a regular occurrence then the need exists to dissect the underlying causes and craft corrective action. Often the majority of causes can be tracked to common basic flaws:

- Inadequate emphasis and resource commitment related to the personnel involved.
- The lack of a structured process, including proper use of the accounting system and a standard payment schedule.
- Inattention to reviewing invoice details such as the open balance due, payment dates, or in matching the invoice to supporting documentation.
- A non-cooperative environment between the personnel performing the payables function and other employees and management responsible for transaction support processing and payment authorization.
- The wrong personnel for the payables task.

Skillful management review of the process to define the problem and its cause, and to create a workable solution, is well worth the time invested. In addition, some specialized peripheral requirements such as year-end 1099 reporting and sales taxes may require external support to set up properly.

Credit and Collections Planning

Problems in the credit and collections process have many parallels to the payables process. However, a few unique areas that scream for attention include the granting of credit and the practicing the "art" of collections.

In regards to the granting of credit – be cautious. Develop clear guidelines about which criteria are acceptable for a given credit level, and who is authorized to grant the credit. If customers clearly cannot pay for the product, they should be filtered out in a proper screening process? Do not get trapped into unauthorized salesman promises, period end must-ship orders, or overextended credit lines with "C" grade customers.

> *In regards to the granting of credit – be cautious.*

The art of collections requires different approaches for different customers. "A" grade customers generally do not pose a credit risk, but with a generally larger credit balance, collections timing can whipsaw a start-up company's cash flow. A few tried and true approaches for tightening the collections cycle with these customers are:

- Negotiating a firm commitment with mutually acceptable penalty clauses as part of the purchase contract. This may still be difficult to enforce.
- Ensuring the marketing/sales function has a mechanism to monitor customer sell through or usage (how much of your product they have actually used as opposed to how much is sitting on their shelf), and that they communicate potential issues with the collections function. You may want to consider paying external sales rep commissions only after collections have occurred.
- Getting to know individuals in the entire processing loop of the customer, and developing the relationship of trust with them

"C" Grade customers generally do pose a credit risk, and therefore proper risk management involves keeping the credit line relatively small, monitoring any balance that is past due or even shortly due, and holding new orders and shipments if the credit line will be exceeded. A periodic discussion with your salesman about the company's relationship with the customer is also a positive step. This discussion should include analysis of the health of the customer's business. One finesse trick some companies use is the promise to be a stellar credit reference if the customer consistently provides the account priority attention (this method can also work between your company and a few select vendors to help maintain your own credit references). If the customer does experience problems, it is often best to try to negotiate a reasonable payment schedule instead of a demand for full and immediate payment.

Payroll

Payroll and the broader general benefits processing functions are two of the most heavily regulated areas of corporate practice. This regulation creates an atmosphere that ends up either in a smooth process or, conversely, a nasty mess.

Because of the heavy regulation several first class payroll processing providers have been able to develop standard systems and provide them for use by companies of all sizes at a reasonable cost. Given the complexities of trying to process payroll internally versus the availability of strong outsourced providers, my choice is clearly for the outsourced provider on a complete "tax pay and file basis."

Under a tax pay and file basis, the outsourced processing agent:
- Collects all funds necessary for net pay along with employee and employer taxes directly from the company's bank account.
- Creates all employee checks and auto deposits.
- Is responsible for all tax deposit and tax return filing requirements.

Some of the outsourced payroll providers I am familiar with include ADP and Paychex, Inc.

Of course, the processing of each payroll is based upon input data supplied by the company – so the retro term of "garbage in, garbage out" remains apropos. If your staff is underexperienced, have them obtain proper training. Insist on the development and maintenance of straightforward company specific documentation of the data input process to prevent a catastrophic employee turnover problem. At the very least all employees take vacation or become ill at some point (an employee in a sensitive function who never takes vacation or calls in ill has a higher potential for hiding fraud).

Stand-alone benefits processing is less well defined as an outsourced function. As a result many start-up companies have not outsourced the function. A good benefits broker will take the time to ensure your staff has the proper forms and processing instructions. In this case the crucial element is to ensure that your broker of choice communicates, is responsive, and stays attuned to the hand-holding needed by under-experienced staff. Therefore not only should a key management member be involved in the selection process, the manager should also schedule a periodic, open update discussion with the benefits broker and your staff.

A workable alternative for some companies is the co-employment arrangement, an arrangement that wraps all employee payroll and benefits processing together and outsources the combined package to a third party. These companies become the actual employer of record for your employees and are often able to provide benefits on par with larger established companies at an equal or lower cost to you. They generally cover their costs and make their profit from the margin obtained through aggregating a larger group of employees to obtain lower benefit costs while charging your company the standard small company benefit rates.

A few co-employment companies have begun to make their mark, but you should thoroughly check out any potential co-employer. Do they specialize in start-ups, how much support will they provide on administrative processing, are they financially stable, will they be onsite, how competitive (cost and coverage) are their benefit plans? Some of the co-employers I am familiar with include Execustaff, Administaff and Ambrose.

> *The processing of each payroll is based upon input data supplied by the company—so the retro term of "garbage in, garbage out" remains apropos.*

Other Functions of the Company

Several other functional areas that are not typically part of accounting and finance nonetheless have significant financial impact on the financial health of the organization. Sales funnel monitoring, purchase order processing, inventory control, engineering project management, engineering and production change orders, and partner contract programs are just a few examples. Ensuring that these functional areas have the same thought development as a prelude to the process creation and process review is therefore smart business sense. Developing appropriate hurdle criteria, exception prevention, process reporting, and management awareness are control steps that apply to all functional areas of the organization. At the very least these items should be included on your company's Authorization Matrix.

Conclusion

A baseline internal financial control system functions as the skeleton and nervous system of your company. Important skeletal elements include authorization limits (e.g. an Authorization Matrix) and a common agreed upon reference guide (e.g. the Chart of Accounts) that outlines company policies and recording conventions. The nervous system of the company works only with reporting of correct, timely and appropriate operational metrics. Incorrect, untimely and missing information leaves management open to negative shocks. Transaction processing problems in receivable, disbursement, payroll and employee benefit processes often must be reviewed to find the true underlying problems in the system.

Seven Hard Learned Lessons

Successfully starting a venture-backed company has a lot in common with poker—the lessons are not cheap. Being a veteran of several start-up companies I have helped pay for some hard learned lessons. With some foresight and luck, you can avoid paying to relearn the following seven lessons.

One - Too Much Ego and Greed

Ego and Greed are prime motivators within the entrepreneur's mind. However, if ego and greed are not checked and controlled, they will undercut your start-up.

A prime example of an unchecked ego occurs when a founder team refuses to bring in the most powerful new members to the management team that they can, or by not giving all members of the management team the authority to perform. Whether this means that a non-founder CEO now leads the management team or that the management team includes specific outside key managers, the failure to check the founder's ego has tanked many start-up companies. Wars are won by placing the best people in their appropriate positions on the battlefield—and giving them the authority to fight the battles.

Greed can often become uncontrolled during negotiations. What is important to achieve during a negotiation process is your major objectives, and to allow the other party to achieve its own. For example, during negotiations to set a company's pre-money valuation, striving to push the valuation upwards by a small percentage can be an unwanted tradeoff for a dirty term sheet riddled with super participating liquidations, full ratchets or excess warrants. Founders will definitely lose on this trade (the venture fund is smarter about financing than you are). The results: now the company has a nasty capitalization structure which will get worse with each successive round; and if the company has a subsequent down-round, or is pressured into a buy-out offer, management will end up with a significantly smaller ownership slice than they bargained for and believe is fair. Always develop a clear understanding of your company's and the other party's major objectives and then focus on their simultaneous achievement.

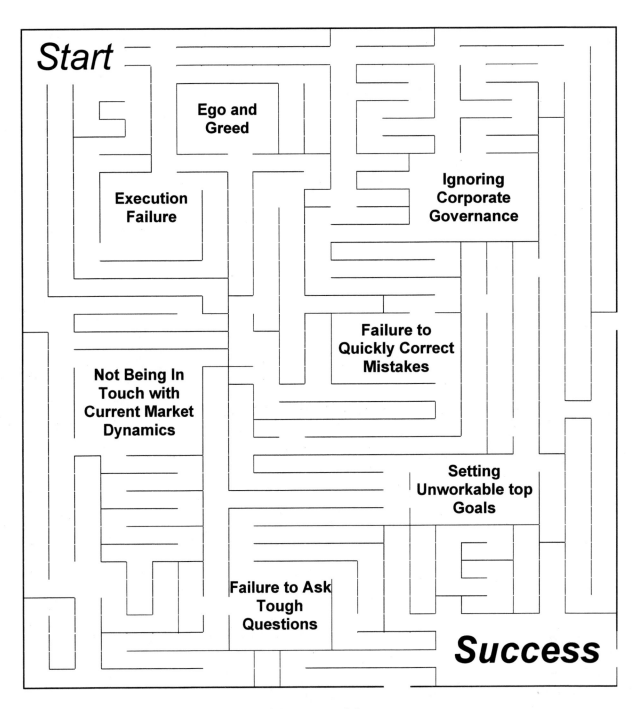

Seven Hard Learned Lessons

Two - Execution Failure

The failure to execute on decisions is at least as bad as not making a decision. How deeply can you pay for the failure to execute effectively?

In one instance, execution failure during the due diligence process resulted in a missed financing. The due diligence process is like an engagement—the company shows its partners an engagement ring and the company is now seen with the venture fund, but the company bank account has not yet grown and a breakup is not yet that expensive (for the venture fund). The company and the venture fund are also probably way beyond first base, and meanwhile, the company cannot ask anyone else out on a date (courtesy of the little "no-shop" clause). The failure to achieve short-term milestones at this stage, as well as a lack of cohesive, gung-ho responses to all due diligence requests is clearly seen as management weakness. The venture fund quietly performs a rapid last minute, no-explanation call off of the wedding.

Another example of execution failure is the perfectionist approach to starting up sales efforts. "We do not have the tools, we do not have the message packaged correctly, and therefore we cannot talk to our prospective customers." Wake up! You have to engage customers who will use your product. Waiting until all the marketing messages are absolutely perfect is a guarantee that your messages are not perfect, and therefore you will have no customers. "Good enough" should get the process started; focus on the delivery of the end results.

> *The due diligence process is like an engagement — the company shows its partners an engagement ring and the company is now seen with the venture fund, but the company bank account has not yet grown and divorce is not yet that expensive (for the venture fund).*

Three - Ignoring Corporate Governance

Corporate Governance is a simple, often overlooked task. Holding regularly scheduled board meetings in which the state of the business is frankly discussed, key goals are reaffirmed, key decisions are agreed upon, and the routine board tasks are set—such as approving option plans and grants, contractual authority, etc.—is a basic requirement.

Consider again the financing process. I have seen companies walk into a financing due diligence phase with over a year's worth of simple unattended board actions to be performed. How much direction do you think the Board of Directors was really giving the company? (Hint: no meetings = no direction) At best this becomes a significant delay on closing the financing round (i.e. the point when *their* money is in *your* bank). At worst the lead investors back out at the final stage. If you're lucky, you'll succeed on closing the round, but only with significantly modified terms.

> *How much direction do you think the Board of Directors was really giving the company? (Hint: no meetings = no direction)*

Another example. You promised your best employee 10,000 options six months ago when she was hired. You had just completed the seed round two days earlier with a $2 per preferred share price. Progress has been stellar, in part due to the performance of that star employee, and now your first venture-round solicitation effort has resulted in a proposed $6 per preferred share price. At the next board meeting, the first in six months, the board determines that the option should be granted at $1 per common share, the current fair market value, compared to $.25 a share for those granted during the seed round. Is your star employee motivated? The company will not obtain any real money from the option price difference, but your star employee receives an unnecessary psychological disappointment. Simple corporate governance is one of the most overlooked, and easiest to correct, weaknesses in many start-ups.

Four - Failure to Quickly Correct Mistakes

All companies, especially start-ups, make mistakes (ergo the theme of this chapter). How often the mistakes get repeated—and how long you live with them—separates the survivors from the names at intellectual property garage sales.

Perhaps you have hired your first salesman—the references were great, the behavioral interviews revealed the candidate as a super salesman, the management team had full buy-in, etc.—now how long will it take you to determine if he or she is able to perform in your company and market space? If your answer is more than three months, you have wasted much more than the hiring bonus, recruiting fees, salary and draw. You have wasted precious evolution time of the company!

Another example of the failure to correct mistakes was in choosing the wrong customer entry segment. One company chose a customer segment that desperately needed the company's product but could not pay. A customer segment that cannot pay for your product or that has an even larger pain elsewhere in their business model is a hard segment to achieve a solid penetration. So if you made a mistake, admit it and correct it now before more lifeblood is sucked out of the company.

Five - Not Being In Touch with Current Market Dynamics

What are the dynamics in your customer's market place today? Are your customers retrenching? Have they been burned by many promises similar to yours that have soured their taste? Do they see a compelling need to invest in new technology like your product? If you do not know the answers, and do not understand how the answers are changing today, then you are not in touch.

Understanding the financial funding market dynamics related to your company is also a key requirement. In 1999, attention was given to companies who planned on spending the fastest in the Internet land rush. Companies that failed to see a shift in the market dynamics before the last quarter of 2000 simply could not raise additional funding — attention was now being given to those companies who showed they could survive and prosper even if no additional funding was brought forth. The market gauge on the perceived value that is placed on your peer companies must be constantly monitored. If you do not know how your private real and perceived competitors' recent financing rounds have fared — and likewise the multiples placed on your public competitors, then you have no business asking a venture fund for money. Keeping in touch is just plain hard work.

Six - Failure to Ask and Answer the Tough Questions

We all like the occasional softball question. But seeking a steady diet of gentle dialogue, which fails to challenge you to think, will set you up for failure when though questions are asked.

> *Seeking a steady diet of gentle dialogue, which fails to challenge you to think, will set you up for failure when though questions are asked.*

For instance, in choosing a consultant for a specific project, are you more likely to engage a consultant who agrees with everything you say, or one who asks fundamental questions that strongly challenge your business plan? The first choice guarantees a status quo business plan. The second choice, while offering no guarantees, gives you the fighting chance to improve your business plan.

Articulating and understanding how your product is better than tomorrow's competition cannot be attained without diligent thought. Provoke those thoughts by seeking out the tough questions, formulating complete answers, and thoroughly testing the answers. The cycle must be repeated over and over. Only then can you articulate with confidence a compelling vision that will survive the tough and challenging questions and respond to them intelligently.

Seven - Setting Unworkable Top Goals

Most venture backed start-up companies recognize that a failure to incorporate top goals will set the company up for failure. However, just setting top goals is not enough. The top goals must take into account the environment within which the company operates and drive every decision of the company.

First, a company's top goals must evolve with the company. As goals are achieved they need to be continually expanded. For example, as you become number one in a targeted entry customer segment, the goal of "being number one in that customer segment" must be replaced with the goal of "leveraging the achievement into being number one in several additional targeted segments."

Some companies fail by setting top goals that require resources and events that are not realistically available to the company now or in the foreseeable future. Several companies have found out the hard way that educating an industry to believe your company has created a completely new market segment is just too expensive for a bootstrap startup. Wiser companies position themselves as "unique" in an established segment and subsequently grow, based on their success, into a new market segment.

The top goals of the company must also cascade down into each decision of the company. For example, a top company goal of a software solutions company may be to become a trusted solution provider. However, if there is not a central management of professional services dedicated to both deployment and user training then the company has not been guided by their top goal in making this decision.

And if there is central management of all related functions, is the central management at the Vice Presidential level? A no answer would indicate another failure to translate the top goal into the decision.

Another common problem in striving to achieve goals is a rationalization of "this was the best we could do" instead of actively developing the strategy of "how do we get to where we need to go." I have heard many more companies say, "This is the best candidate we could sign on," then I have heard say, "We targeted the best candidate and strategized how to engage him or her."

> *The top goals of the company must also cascade down into each decision of the company.*

Conclusion

These lessons and the examples used to illustrate them are by no means an exhaustive list of all the mistakes start-up companies can and will commit. However, a company that recognizes and avoids habitual commission of these seven mistakes has taken significant steps towards becoming a successful company.

Hints for solving the maze:
- *There is often more than one solution to the problem.*
- *There are a lot of up and downs and sideways movements on the path to success.*
- *There are many dead ends and blind alleys.*
- *There is more than one way to fall into most traps.*
- *You must sometimes think outside of the box.*

Index

Appendix A - Chronological Index to Graphs, Tables, Charts